Undone:

A Life Application Journey through Isaiah

Candle Sutton

Introduction

I love the prophets. I know, weird, huh? But I do. God has given me a love for these mysterious, and often difficult, books and shows me how they apply to our lives today.

That's what I hope to share with you through this study.

If you've come here hoping to hear all the answers and unlock every ancient mystery in this deep book of prophecy, you're in the wrong place. Frankly, I don't think you'll ever find that this side of Heaven.

But if you've come here to study God's word and be challenged in your faith, then read on.

You'll find this study broken down by chapter (with a few exceptions), with questions that I hope will engage your heart, mind, and soul.

The first question will always direct you to consider the chapter as a whole, so I'd encourage you to read through the entire chapter before focusing in on the application questions. Looking at the chapter in its entirety helps provide a sense of continuity that you might otherwise miss.

After each lesson, I'll include a brief summary of some of the things God said to me, as well as information I found when researching the book. I use the New Living Translation and the NIV so if the wording in your Bible doesn't quite line up with mine, don't worry – the basic meaning should still be the same.

Pray and ask God to reveal more of Himself to you. Then be prepared for Him to do just that as you study His word. Remember that when it comes to studying God's word, you'll only get out as much as you're willing to put into it, so turn off your phone, set aside the time, and really enjoy fellowship with our personal Lord.

I pray you will be as blessed by the book of Isaiah as I have been.

The Setting

There are many different opinions on the book of Isaiah, not all of them Biblically based. I won't get into them here, but will focus on the facts as they are presented in the Bible.

Chapter 6 gives the story of God's commission to Isaiah to be His prophet. Why doesn't the commission appear in chapter 1? I don't know. Perhaps the events of chapters 1-5 occurred before God specifically called Isaiah into service. Or perhaps God called Isaiah to put those chapters first. The sequence of events isn't really what's important here. What matters most is the message God delivers through His prophet.

It's in chapter 6 that we learn that Isaiah saw a vision of God in the year that King Uzziah died. It is believed that Uzziah died in 740 B.C. Isaiah 1:1 tells us that Isaiah's ministry lasted during the reign of four kings: Uzziah, Jotham, Ahaz, and Hezekiah. You can find their stories starting in 2 Kings 15.

The short version is that Uzziah and Jotham are recorded as having done "what was right in the eyes of the Lord", yet they failed to remove the idolatrous high places and pagan altars throughout the land. Because of this, there was no spiritual reform and idolatry continued to run rampant throughout the nation.

Ahaz was a wicked king who sacrificed his own children to false gods, shut up the Lord's temple, and built altars in every town.

Hezekiah is the shining star among the group. Not only did he do what was right before the Lord, he initiated widespread spiritual reform, restoring proper worship of God, repairing the temple, destroying pagan altars and inspiring the people to destroy their own personal idols. He illustrates the influence a true, godly leader can have on the people he leads and should prompt all of us to consider the example we set to those around us.

Not much is known about Isaiah himself, nor does Isaiah tell us much about himself in his book. Rather, his focus is on God and the messages God gave him. It seems as though his calling as prophet was common knowledge in his day, for he appears to have had easy access to the kings (Isaiah 7, 38) and Hezekiah sought out Isaiah during times of distress. The exact end date of his ministry is also unknown, although it may have lasted as late as 681 B.C.

This was a time of great turmoil in the land. Assyria was quickly rising to power and conquering nations all around Israel and Judah. Israel itself fell around 722 B.C. Judah held out longer, but eventually fell into captivity as well, with Jerusalem falling around 586 B.C., during Jeremiah's ministry.

It's hard for us to imagine the fear and distress surrounding the people during this time, but I'd encourage you to try. War is all around you. Nations have fallen. Your enemy grows larger, seemingly by the day. Attacks can come at any time. Spies are everywhere. Food and water are in high demand and short supply. And out of this, you have a prophet calling you to repent because this is God's judgment against your sin.

Some repeated themes in the book of Isaiah are sin (specifically idolatry), repentance, judgment, and mercy. There are many places that point to the coming Messiah, His rule, and the benefits He brings, such as right standing with God.

So read on. And expect God to change you as you spend time with Him in His word.

Isaiah 1

1. From this chapter, what impresses, stands out, or convicts you?

2. Isaiah 1:1-3
   a. What truths about Israel are revealed in these verses?

   b. What examples come to mind of how we are guilty of this same ignorance today?

3. Isaiah 1:4-9
   a. What were the results of the people's rejection of Almighty God?

   b. What warnings and evidences of mercy do you see as our country continues to reject God?

   c. What problem, struggles, or pain in your life might be a

result of disobedience?

4. Isaiah 1:10-15
   a. Why was God rejecting the sacrifices He had previously directed the people to present?

   b. In what ways do Christians today corrupt the worship of God?

   c. What sin in your life might be hindering your prayers?

5. Isaiah 1:16-20
   a. How do these verses reveal God's tender heart toward His sinful people?

   b. What practical steps can you take today to follow the Lord's directions?

6. Isaiah 1:21-31
   a. What are some modern examples of the charges God brought against His people?

b. What blessings did God promise His judgment would bring?

c. In what ways have you experienced God's refining in your own life?

Chapter 1 – Thoughts and Considerations

One of the golden rules of writing is that you have to hook your readers at the very beginning. It's no coincidence that God does this very thing in the first chapter of Isaiah.

Verse 1 introduces the prophet and establishes the specific time in history, but God gets right down to business in verse 2, where He calls both heaven and earth as witnesses to what He is about to say. There are some interesting points to consider about this.

First of all, God's two "witnesses" are significant; the heavens would typically include the sky, sun, moon, and stars – so, technically, everything above mankind that would have a birds-eye view of what happens on earth – and the earth, which would include everything around mankind and the environment in which we live. God's two witnesses are all encompassing and would have seen and experienced the effects of the sins God will soon expose.

Secondly, the Mosaic Law required a minimum of two witnesses for a testimony to be valid (Deuteronomy 19:15). Now, obviously, God has no need of witnesses, for His testimony is always valid, but I love the way He meets us where we're at. The people (like us) had deviated seriously off course and God was using whatever means necessary to draw them back to Himself.

Isn't it interesting how God compares His rebellious people to common work animals? He even goes so far as to say that those animals are smarter than His people, for at least they know to whom they belong. When we look at those two animals, a few things pop out: oxen are built for labor and are not known for moving very quickly (much like God's people when He calls them to repent) and donkeys are known for being stubborn.

Personally, I see strong symbolism in the animals God chose to name here.

The following verses really highlight the damaging effects of sin. The people are loaded with a burden of guilt, injured, sick, and battered; the land is in ruins, burned, plundered, destroyed, abandoned, and helpless. Yet in verses 9-10, we see God's mercy as He purposefully spares people and urges them to come back to Him.

Verses 10-15 contain a warning that I feel is particularly relevant to us today.

God condemns their religious practices.

Why? Because they were merely going through the motions. It reminds me of what many people do today. We go to church for show or because of some kind of legalistic reason – maybe even in a vain attempt to earn "brownie points" with God. At church, we sing songs without thinking about what we're saying, we listen to the sermon while thinking about what we're going to do after church or later that week, maybe we even read the Bible or pray, but do so out of ritual or to mark it off some kind of worthless checklist.

I know that last point is something I have to constantly guard against. With what attitude do you approach these things? Now obviously I'm not telling you to stop going to church or reading the Bible, but I think it's important that we check our attitudes and motives. The body of Christ needs to have Christ as its focus.

God presents the solution in verses 16-20. He calls them to turn to Him, to leave their sinful ways behind, to cling to His mercy, and to let Him make them "white as snow."

With that, God gives them some very specific actions to take – mostly involving their treatment of the most vulnerable members of their society: the oppressed, orphans, and widows. In the male-dominated Biblical times, members of these groups not only had no rights, they were often overlooked and destitute. Modern times have changed that, but we still have vulnerable groups that need our love and compassion. A few that come to my mind are the homeless, mentally or physically challenged, kids in foster care, the abused, single parents or children in single parent households, the elderly, or shut-ins. I'm sure you can think of others to add to that list and likely even have specific names and faces to attach to some of them.

God closes this chapter by showing how His once-holy people are now defiled, His prized possession is now worthless. He seems to put special emphasis on the wicked leadership the people have followed.

But don't you love the merciful promises God makes here? He promises an end to their troubles, that He will establish just and wise leadership, that He will restore Jerusalem, and that evil will be destroyed.

What an amazingly loving and just God we have!

Isaiah 2

1. From this chapter, what impresses, stands out, or convicts you?

2. Isaiah 2:1-5

   a. In what ways do you think this prophecy has been fulfilled already? In what ways do you think the fulfillment is still future to us?

   b. What truths do you believe God has been teaching you recently and for what purpose?

   c. How willing are you to walk the path God has chosen for you when it differs from your plans?

3. Isaiah 2:6-8

   a. What do you think Isaiah meant by "You have abandoned Your people"?

   b. What are some examples of each of these sins in our culture today?

c. Which of your customs or practices might be detestable to the Lord?

4. Isaiah 2:9-17

   a. What are some things our culture worships or glorifies?

   b. Who do you live to exalt – yourself or God? Would God say the same thing?

5. Isaiah 2:17-21

   a. How does an unbeliever's dread of the Lord differ from a believer's fear of the Lord?

   b. What are some examples of idols in our day? What idols exist in your own life?

6. Isaiah 2:22

   a. In what or whom does our culture trust? Where do you place your trust?

Chapter 2 – Thoughts and Considerations

What a glorious day it will be when we see the events of verses 1-4 fulfilled! I see partial fulfillments already, but the ultimate peace described in verse 4 is still future to us.

I love the eagerness of the people described here – they are anxious to be taught by God and to walk in His ways. Personally, I feel like parts of these verses were moderately fulfilled during the days Jesus walked the earth – certainly people from many nations sought Jesus out and listened to Him as He told them of God and God's kingdom. Jesus' teaching did go out from Jerusalem, but not to the extent that it one day will.

By contrast, it is so sobering that in verse 6 we see that God rejected His people.

You might be wondering how this can be. God is loving, after all. The important thing to remember here is that it was the *people*, not God, who broke the covenant (see Exodus 19). They traded Almighty God for worthless idols so, as Romans 1:21-32 tells us, God gave them over to the sin they so desired. It was the *people* who persisted in sin, despite the countless prophets and warnings God sent to turn them back. It was the *people* who filled their land with sorcery, idolatry, and pride.

Pride. It's a recurring theme in the prophets. I've always felt like pride is the root of all sin. Pride says that my way is better than God's. Pride says that I'm more important than God. Therefore, pride is good at justifying everything God says is wrong.

God will not share the glory that is rightly due to Him with anyone else (Isaiah 42:8, 48:11) so He will humble all those who exalt themselves.

What a warning this is for us. When we exalt ourselves, we take the place that should belong to God alone. Who can stand against

God? No one. In fact, we see in verse 19 that God's enemies try to hide when He acts. More than that, they will finally realize the futility of their idols and abandon them in their haste to escape God's just judgment.

I love how this chapter ends. God sums it up nicely with a warning and a hypothetical question: "Don't put your trust in mere humans. They are as frail as breath. What good are they?" (NLT)

As easy as it is to pin our hopes on a good leader, a loved one, family member, or friend, God promises that they can't save us. In fact, at some point they will let us down – it's human nature.

But God will never let us down.

He alone is worthy of our utmost confidence. Where have you chosen to place your trust?

Isaiah 3-4

1.From these chapters, what impresses, stands out, or convicts you?

2.Isaiah 3:1-3
   a. Why do you think the Lord took these things away?

   b. In what ways is our society guilty of these same attitudes?

   c. How have these attitudes infiltrated your own life?

3.Isaiah 3:4-15
   a. What are some of the characteristics of bad leadership highlighted in these verses?

   b. In what ways do you see some of the same things happening today?

   c. Whom has God called you to lead? What might God need

to change in you to make your leadership more effective?

4. Isaiah 3:16-4:1
   a. Do you think this message was literally for the women or were the women being used figuratively?

   b. What charges and consequences did the Lord bring against the women of Zion?

   c. What specific examples of these same things do you see in our society today?

5. Isaiah 4:2-6
   a. To what or whom do you think "the Branch of the Lord" refers?

   b. How does God's judgment on believers differ from His judgment on unbelievers?

   c. In what trials are you currently seeking shelter or refuge from someone other than the Lord?

d. For what promises or blessings will you thank God today?

Chapters 3 and 4 – Thoughts and Considerations

In looking at these chapters, I think it's important to look back at the end of chapter 2. God warned His people against trusting in humans. In the first 3 verses of chapter 3, God lists some of the things in which people place their trust and warns them that He will strip all of it away until they are left with no one but Him.

I think sometimes it's easy to read this and gloss right over it by thinking we are placing our trust in God, but let's take a step back, because this applies to us as well.

If I were to ask you about the last presidential election, how would you respond? Did you get all passionate and worked up about one candidate over the other? Did you engage in dirty back-biting, name-calling behavior as so many people did? When the results were announced, did you feel that our country had been saved or was doomed because of the candidate who won?

I'm not saying we shouldn't care about politics or who is running our country – because we absolutely should – but we must be careful to not pin our hopes on our leaders. Only God won't ever let us down and He alone is to be our ultimate hope and help.

In fact, 3:4-15 highlight the importance of good leadership. Without it, cities decay and countries fall. These verses make it clear that God will hold leaders accountable for how they lead, so we should all examine our lives carefully. You undoubtedly hold a leadership position somewhere – perhaps in your home or with your children, perhaps at your job, perhaps in your church, maybe even in an online community – seek God and follow Him as you lead so that your actions will be in line with what He says is right. We can see from this passage (as well as others), that the example we set for those around us matters.

Verses 10-11 drive this point home. Both the righteous and the wicked are promised that they will reap the consequences of their actions.

I wanted to point out the cultural element in verse 12 for just a second. Maybe you chafed at the negative implications of young or female leaders. In reading Scripture, it's always important to remember the context in which it was written. Culturally, in those days, following children or women was unacceptable.

However, we can see from the life of Jesus that God doesn't view women or children as second-class citizens. In fact, Jesus spent time with both groups, often defending them against those who would seek to criticize or oppress them. He also spoke favorably about both groups on numerous occasions. See Matthew 18:1-19:15, Mark 14:1-9, and John 8:1-11 for just a few examples.

Isaiah 3:16-4:1 give quite the image of Jerusalem as she is personified as a beautiful woman! Personally, I doubt this warning was only for the women. Rather, I see it as a warning against seeking the perishable. The "woman" mentioned here spent great time and effort making herself beautiful, but it would all be stripped away on the day of judgment.

Here, again, it's important to think about the cultural setting for the original audience. Family was of great importance and being single was highly undesirable – hence the disgrace mentioned in verse 1. Women had few rights and, often, little value in that society so her ability to provide heirs for her husband was commonly a measure of her worth. Now the life of Christ proves that God does not devalue women that way (you know, in case you needed some proof), however in that time and society, it was the social norm.

4:2-6 provides a rich contrast to the judgment in chapter 3! You'll find this to be a reoccurring pattern in Isaiah – passages of judgment followed by promises of mercy and blessing. God's judgment is a fearful thing for unbelievers, but for Christians, judgment is beneficial.

Verse 4 talks about God cleansing Jerusalem with His judgment. God often uses judgment to reveal our sin. If we allow God to purge sin from our lives, we can anticipate His blessings to follow.

It seems likely that the "Branch of the Lord" is a reference to Jesus the Messiah, but there are other opinions on this matter – and possibly multiple meanings. It might refer to the remnant that God saves, it could refer to Judah as a nation, or even to some sect of people that is not named specifically. The point is that God's cleansing will bring about the holiness He desires and He will protect, provide for, and restore His people.

Isaiah 5

1. From this chapter, what impresses, stands out, or convicts you?

2. Isaiah 5:1-7
   a. In what ways had God demonstrated His love for His people?

   b. How has God's past care of you proven the depth of His love?

   c. What good fruit is evidenced in your life? In what areas might bad fruit be creating a stench to God?

3. Isaiah 5:8-10
   a. What are some modern examples of this sin in our culture today?

4. Isaiah 5:11-17
   a. What are some modern examples of these sins in our culture today?

b. What might be the root cause of all these sins?

5. Isaiah 5:18-19
   a. What do you think God is saying in this woe? What would be some modern examples?

6. Isaiah 5:20-21
   a. How do you see these evidenced in our culture today?

7. Isaiah 5:22-23
   a. What are some modern examples of these sins in our culture today?

   b. Prayerfully consider all 6 woes. In what areas of your life do you see any of these attitudes or sins manifested?

8. Isaiah 5:24-30
   a. Why would this disaster come upon them?

   b. What evidences of judgment do you see in our nation today?

Chapter 5 – Thoughts and Considerations

This chapter starts with a stark contrast, doesn't it? God portrays Himself as a gardener, lovingly tending the crop He planted.

If you know your Old Testament history, it's easy to see the parallels here. God chose Abraham, made him into a nation, then gave His people a beautiful land "overflowing with milk and honey" (Exodus 3:8).

He "dug it up" by giving the Israelites victory in battle and driving the other nations from the land. In doing so, he also "cleared it of stones" – things that would hold them back or hinder them, such as enemy nations and the idolatry so rampant in those days. He "planted the choicest vines" by giving them the law, which – like a vine – would provide the essential spiritual nourishment they needed to live holy lives.

Finally, He built a watchtower to safeguard the people – the temple and priests, who would intercede for the people for forgiveness of sins. I'd add the prophets God sent as part of this watchtower, for they were God's instruments of warning when danger (typically unchecked sin) threatened the people.

But in spite of all God had done, the people rebelled, growing like wild grapes – or even weeds – in the place God had so carefully constructed.

The verses that follow highlight some of their specific sins. The six woes show the condition of the people's hearts.

To get the full impact, I think we need to look beneath the surface of the words to the attitudes that sparked the sins listed.

The first woe (vs. 8-10) – buying up houses and land – sounds like good business sense, right?

However for God to call this out as a sin, it's likely that the people were being materialistic and greedy, perhaps to the detriment of others. If you check out the cross-reference verses, you'll find Micah 2:2, which speaks of gaining land through dishonest means and robbing families of their rightful inheritance. If you look at God's original direction regarding land ownership (Leviticus 25:8-24), you find that land was supposed to be returned to the original family in the year of jubilee. Leviticus 25:23 really drives it home – "The land must not be sold permanently because the land is Mine, and you are but aliens and My tenants." To me, this implies that the land owners were not adhering to God's laws, making them guilty of far more than only greed.

The second woe (vs. 11-12) lists several sins: drunkenness, partying, and – most importantly "they never think about the Lord or notice what He is doing." I think it's easy for some of us to read that and think that it's not applicable because we don't drink (or maybe only drink occasionally and in moderation, depending upon your personal standards), but I think this woe covers more than alcohol. I see this woe as pertaining to all worldliness, the pursuit of pleasure at any cost, and indifference to God. When we broaden the scope and look at the heart attitude, it hits a little closer to home, doesn't it?

The third woe (vs. 18-19) can be a little confusing, depending upon your translation. Sometimes it helps me to look at multiple translations to see if I can gain a broader picture. The NLT says "drag their sins behind them with ropes made of lies, who drag wickedness behind them like a cart", NIV "draw sin along with cords of deceit, and wickedness as with cart ropes", GWT "string people along with lies and empty promises, whose lives are sinful," GNT "unable to break free from your sins," and NKJ "draw iniquity with cords of vanity, and sin as if with a cart rope." In looking at all these translations, there are several possible interpretations: people who are stuck in sin who may – or may not – want to turn from it; people who eagerly and actively pursue sin with no regard for right or wrong; people who purposely lead others astray with lies and empty promises.

We also see a blatant defiance toward God, perhaps to the

point of agnosticism or atheism (verse 19). Not only do these people think God won't act, I feel like it's implied that they believe God *can't* act, like He isn't powerful enough to do what He says He will do. This verse, to me anyway, implies that these people openly challenge God's power and authority.

The fourth woe (vs. 20) mentions people who call what is evil good and what is good evil. If done intentionally, these are people who love sin more than righteousness – which is especially dangerous because they will likely deceive and mislead others.

We see this all around us in the world today. People justify what the Bible clearly defines as sin so that they can continue on in it and – using worldly logic – convince others that they are right. This is why studying the Bible is so important; it alone provides a standard to which we can measure the messages we hear for truth.

The fifth woe (vs. 21) is directed at those who are "wise in their own eyes" and think they're so clever. It hits at what I believe to be the heart of our sin condition – pride.

The sixth woe (vs. 22-23) again looks at alcohol and loose living, but also touches on injustice. Possibly the core issue of this woe is corruption, misplaced values, and those who glorify sin.

The chapter concludes with the consequences of unchecked sin – judgment.

Do you struggle with the idea that God would act in such a seemingly harsh manner?

Trust me, I do, too. For me, it's hard to reconcile the grace He's shown me with the judgment described in the books of prophecy. But it's important to remember how many warnings He issued – even here, He's warning them, through the words of Isaiah, to turn before the judgment falls.

I think the key verse to keep in mind here is found in the latter part of verse 24 – "For they have rejected the law of the Lord of Heaven's armies; they have despised the word of the Holy One of Israel."

The people weren't just living in ignorance. No, they purposefully chose to reject God's words, rejecting Him in the process. In spite of all He did for them and the many, many warnings He'd issued, they continued to blatantly disregard His standards and ignore His holiness.

God's judgment is never rash or abrupt. He never "snaps" or acts out in anger as we do. His judgment is actually justice... and the greater wonder is not that He acts in justice, but that He so frequently withholds the judgment we all deserve.

That, my friends, is His amazing mercy.

Isaiah 6

1. From this chapter, what impresses, stands out, or convicts you?

2. Isaiah 6:1-4
   a. What most impacts you about Isaiah's vision of the Lord?

   b. Isaiah says He saw the Lord, yet in Exodus 33:20 God tells Moses that no one can see Him and live. How would you explain this seeming inconsistency?

   c. How does your view of God compare to Isaiah's vision? In what ways might you have minimized God or His holiness?

3. Isaiah 6:5-7
   a. Why do you think Isaiah lamented his unclean lips and not his meditations, actions, or sin in general?

   b. What do you think is the significance of a burning or live coal being used as God's instrument of cleansing?

c. What sin in your life has God revealed to you as you've studied His holiness in this passage?

4. Isaiah 6:8-10

a. What is especially significant to you from these verses as Isaiah hears God's call and responds?

b. What might be the reason or motivation for Isaiah's eager response to God's call?

c. To what areas of service do you sense God calling you? Where are you resisting His call?

5. Isaiah 6:11-13

a. In light of verses 9-10, what does Isaiah's question tell you about him and his faith in God?

b. How does your attitude compare to Isaiah's when God says something you don't want to hear?

c. What hope does God provide Isaiah?

d. In what ways has God given you hope or encouragement in the midst of difficult circumstances?

Chapter 6 – Thoughts and Considerations

I love this chapter! Isaiah's call vividly highlights God's greatness, His majesty, His holiness, and our need for cleansing.

As I mentioned in the introduction, it's believed that this occurred somewhere around 740 B.C. The fact that Isaiah tells us that it's in the year that King Uzziah died gives a very definite time for the vision.

There are a few options I came up with that might explain how Isaiah "saw" God. It's possible that he actually saw Jesus before Jesus' incarnation. Or maybe God's face was out of view or obscured by light or smoke. Also, if this was a vision or a dream, then Isaiah didn't physically see God. There are likely many other possible explanations, but those are the ones that immediately came to my mind.

As I thought about the train of God's robe filling the temple, I was struck by how big God is. The temple was a massive structure and if just the train of God's robe filled it, that's a pretty big robe. When I think about God, I have this horrible tendency to try to shrink him down to my size. It's probably because my mind can't comprehend how large God is, but to shrink him down is to risk creating a false god, for that's not the God we see in Scripture. Where do you have an inaccurate picture of God?

It's interesting to me how Isaiah's immediate response to seeing God is to cry "I am ruined!" (NIV). I am particularly fond of the wording in the King James Version, however, when Isaiah says that he is undone – hence the title of this book.

Have you ever thought about what would happen if you could see God? I doubt saying that we're ruined or undone would immediately come to any of our minds, yet that is how Isaiah responded. He saw God in all His holiness and realized his own sinful, deficient state. Instinctively, he knew he would never be the same. His comment about unclean lips reminded me of Matthew 12:34 – "Out of the overflow of the heart, the mouth speaks." Our words reveal what's inside.

The burning coal could point to the sacrificial system, where the sacrifices were burned to atone for sin. I also wondered if it didn't symbolize the fire of trials that God often uses to expose and purge sin from our lives.

Did you notice that God did not distinctly call Isaiah? Instead, He *asked* who would go. And Isaiah couldn't volunteer fast enough.

I was struck by how little information Isaiah had.

God didn't give him a road map for what was ahead. Isaiah didn't ask God what the mission was or how it would end before volunteering. Isaiah, having seen God and experienced the cleansing God offered, couldn't wait to do what God called him to do. When we have problems serving God, maybe it's because we've forgotten all God has done for us and who He is.

After Isaiah volunteers, God gives him a glimpse of the struggles he would face as he spoke to the people. The people wouldn't understand, would have hard hearts, would choose to not listen or see, and therefore would not receive God's healing.

If God told me that my life's work would amount to all that, I'd probably be asking Him for a new mission; or, at the very least, why He would even have me do something so seemingly pointless.

But did you notice Isaiah's question? He didn't ask for a plan B. He just asked God "how long?"

Isaiah had complete confidence that God's way was right. It's also important to note that Isaiah didn't back down. He was ready to do God's work, regardless of the outcome.

Following the discouraging news of what was to come, God offers the promise of better times. The trials would make the nation holy. It's possible that the "holy seed" refers to the Messiah, but personally, I think the promise is broader and includes the faithful of the nation – from which Messiah would come. God would wipe out their wickedness, leaving a people ready to acknowledge and worship Him.

So if you feel the coal of trials on your "lips" right now, embrace it. It's not an easy thing to do, but God might be purging something from your life so you are ready to do His will.

Isaiah 7

1. From this chapter, what impresses, stands out, or convicts you?

2. Isaiah 7:1-9
   a. What do you think Isaiah purposed to do in pointing out that "the head of Damascus is only Rezin (v 8)... the head of Samaria is only Remaliah's son" (v 9)?

   b. Why do you think God followed the promise of Aram's & Israel's defeat with the admonishment "If you do not stand firm in your faith, you will not stand at all"?

   c. What are some practical examples of ways you can stand firm in your faith today?

3. Isaiah 7:10-13
   a. Deuteronomy 6:16 says not to test God, something Jesus echoes in Matthew 4:7. Why was Ahaz's refusal to ask for a sign displeasing to God?

   b. What are some examples of people in our culture

misconstruing Scripture or hiding sin behind a mask of false piety?

   c. In what areas of your life might you be trying God's patience through disbelief or stubborn disobedience?

4. Isaiah 7:14-16
   a. Why should this sign have been a tremendous encouragement to Isaiah's audience?

   b. Which of God's promises gives you the greatest hope and peace as you face the giants in your life?

5. Isaiah 7:17-25
   a. How would you summarize this prophecy?

   b. Why would God allow such devastation to befall His people?

   c. How do you see our country following these same fateful patterns?

d. What struggles in your life might be the result of God's loving discipline? In what circumstances might God be warning you to turn from sin now?

Chapter 7 – Thoughts and Considerations

These were scary times!

Aram and Israel had aligned together, intent on attacking Judah. 2 Kings 16 and 2 Chronicles 18 provide the historical accounts of this time. In Isaiah 7, we find Isaiah encouraging Ahaz to trust in God, not man; yet we find in the historical accounts that Ahaz turned to Assyria for help.

The great irony here is that Assyria – whom Ahaz was trusting to save him – would later attack Judah and capture all the fortified cities except Jerusalem (Isaiah 36:1). Historians have placed the events of this chapter around 735-734 B.C.

It's important to remember that Ahaz was a wicked king, not a God-follower.

Yet, in spite of that, God pursues Ahaz and encourages him to not only trust God, but goes so far as to invite him to ask for a sign. Ahaz refuses. He hides it behind a mask of false piety "I will not ask, neither will I tempt the Lord." On the surface, it sounds like Ahaz is being obedient to what God had previously commanded in Deuteronomy 6:16, but God knows the heart.

How often we do that! We say the "right" things, but our hearts are not in the right place.

I love how God contrasts the efforts of these kings against the power of Almighty God. He essentially reminds Ahaz that these kings are mere men and Ahaz has God on his side. Unfortunately, the truth doesn't penetrate Ahaz's hard heart.

Ironically, Israel and Aram, the nations of which Ahaz was so afraid, fell to Assyria only a few years later.

I love the last part of verse 9 and think it's one we should all take to heart: "If you do not stand firm in your faith, you will not stand at all."

God alone is our solid foundation. Faith in God strengthens us. Without it, the storms of life beat us down, just like Jesus said in the parable of the wise and foolish builders in Matthew 7:24-27.

The promised sign in verses 14-16 have been a source of debate. While verse 14 clearly points to Jesus Christ, verses 15-16 have a more immediate feel. It's possible there are multiple fulfillments of this prophecy. Culturally, a boy around 12-13 years old was considered to be of age to distinguish right from wrong.

The prophecy in verses 17-25 seemed to me to indicate that an enemy – Assyria – would swarm the country like insects. In those days, hair was very important, so the forced shaving in verse 20 would be horribly embarrassing and disgraceful. The land itself would become desolate, inhabitable only by animals.

God's discipline of His people would strip away everything in which they trusted until He was their only option. What a warning this is to us! When we worship the created rather than the Creator, God will use any means necessary to draw us back to Himself. He wants – and deserves – first place in our hearts, and won't settle for anything less.

Isaiah 8

1. From this chapter, what impresses, stands out, or convicts you?

2. Isaiah 8:1-10
   a. What could the waters of Shiloah symbolize?

   b. What warning and promise is contained in the river metaphor?

   c. What can you do to remember that God is with you when the floods come in your own life?

3. Isaiah 8:11-13
   a. Why might Isaiah have been tempted to follow the ways, conspiracies, or fears of the people?

   b. How would you explain fearing or dreading the Lord to an unbeliever or new Christian?

    c. Into which philosophies or worldly concerns have you been drawn?

4. Isaiah 8:14-15
    a. How can God be both a sanctuary and a stumbling stone?

5. Isaiah 8:16-18
    a. What do you think is meant by the instruction to bind up the testimony and seal up the law?

    b. How does waiting for the Lord demonstrate real trust in Him?

    c. In what current situation are you struggling to wait on the Lord?

6. Isaiah 8:19-22
    a. To what or whom does our culture turn for answers or directions?

b. How would you tie verse 19 to verses 20-22?

c. In what areas of your life have you allowed worldly thinking to dim your vision?

Chapter 8 – Thoughts and Considerations

We get a rare look into the personal life of Isaiah in the opening verses of this chapter. We find out that he was married to a prophetess and that they had a son (we'll later learn they had at least two). With that, God also warns that before the child – presumably this child Isaiah's wife has just borne – can say "my father/mother" both Damascus and Samaria would fall to the Assyrians. Obviously children all develop at an individual rate, but to me this indicates that these events would occur within a year or two of the child's birth. That's a pretty definite and immediate timeframe!

I love the imagery of the waters in verses 6-8 and feel there's a lot we can learn from it.

To me, those gentle waters might refer to God, who promised His people peace and prosperity if they would simply follow Him. As I thought about gently flowing waters, I also thought about how there can be powerful undercurrents just beneath the surface and realized God is the same way. To those of us who know Him, He often deals so gently with us, yet we know His power and ability to work are limitless.

Because they refused this pleasing water, God would unleash upon them a raging river – the mighty Assyria – who would sweep into the land, wipe everything away, and leave death and destruction in its wake.

The tragic thing is that King Ahaz was looking to Assyria for help. Ahaz recognized Assyria's power, much like we recognize the power of a mighty river.

The problem is that rivers are unpredictable.

Just as rivers can overflow their banks and go wherever they please, so Assyria would flood Judah with its tyranny.

Did you catch the hope and promise in verse 8, though? Yes, the water would flow, but it would only go up to the neck. It would be high and dangerous, but it would not completely overtake them. Even then, God would be in perfect control. Water is a cleansing agent and God would use it (specifically Assyria, in this case) to discipline and cleanse His people.

Verse 10 warns about simply relying upon the counsel of man. Man's plans and wisdom come to nothing apart from God.

I love the warning against buying into the fears, conspiracies, and threats of the world. How we need to hear this message today! In the chaos of this world and the information overload that inundates us with all that is going wrong, God calls us to fix our eyes upon Him in trust.

Did you wonder about the instruction to bind and seal the words of God in verse 16?

It's possible that God wasn't instructing Isaiah to seal it so it would be inaccessible; rather the instruction could have more to do with retaining the original message and meaning. When a scroll was bound and sealed, it prevented tampering and showed the document's value and trustworthiness. It might have also been a warning not to add anything to, nor take anything away from, the words God had spoken, a warning that's echoed at the end of the Bible in Revelation 22:18-19.

The chapter ends with a warning about the occult, telling people not to turn to mediums or psychics for help or answers. It makes a very valid point: why would the living consult the dead for help with life? Yet we find that people still do it today. They consult horoscopes or psychics before making a decision when, really, God alone should be consulted.

The constant stream of messages we hear should be weighed against God's word, which is the ultimate truth. If there is discord between the two, go with God's word, for the other will lead you astray.

Isaiah 9:1~10:4

1. From these chapters, what impresses, stands out, or convicts you?

2. Isaiah 9:1-7
   a. In what ways did the coming of Christ enlarge the nation and shatter the burdens of the people?

   b. Do you think the prophecies of verse 7 are to be taken literally, spiritually, or both? Why?

   c. In what areas of your life do you need to surrender to Christ's Lordship today?

3. Isaiah 9:8-12
   a. How does verse 10 reveal the sinful pride of the nation?

   b. In what present situation are you trusting in yourself, others, or things rather than trusting in God?

4. Isaiah 9:13-17

    a. What is significant about the mention of the fatherless and the widows in verse 17?

    b. What seem to be the main causes of the ungodliness, wickedness, and vileness spoken of in verse 17?

    c. To whom do you look for leadership? How do they compare to the leaders described in verses 15-16?

    d. What kind of example are you setting to the people around you?

5. Isaiah 9:18-21

    a. In what ways do you see this happening in our society today?

    b. How might you be guilty of "devouring" someone God has called you to love?

6. Isaiah 10:1-4

    a. How do you see these sins at work in modern society?

    b. Where are you allowing injustice? For whom might God be calling you to take a stand?

Chapter 9:1~10:4 ~ Thoughts and Considerations

Here we find another chapter (plus 4 verses) of contrasts! It begins with the wonderful promises of Messiah, yet ends with warnings of judgment.

Verses 1-7 are often quoted at Christmas, since they point to the coming of Christ, His ministry, and His eventual rule. When I look at these verses, I get the sense that we've yet to see the complete fulfillment of them. The shattering of burdens and removal of oppression (verse 4) and the abolishment of war (verse 5) have certainly not been literally completed; although an argument could be made for a spiritual completion, since we have complete freedom in Christ through the cross.

Even at that, I believe the day is coming when we will see a complete and total fulfillment of these verses – literally – as Jesus establishes His righteous kingdom across the earth and all evil and injustice are forever banished.

Verse 8 marks a drastic shift. We see the attitudes of the people in the face of God's just judgment. They have not learned from the punishment; rather, they arrogantly boast that they will rebuild a better country than the one they lost, using superior products.

You might be asking "What's so bad about that?"

It's not the rebuilding, nor wanting to use quality materials, that's wicked. The answer is in verse 13 – "the people will still not repent. They will not seek the Lord…" The people planned to do everything in their own strength. There's no mention of consulting the Lord or seeking His will.

So God vowed to remove their leaders (presumably wicked), as well as the false prophets – two groups in whom the people would place their trust. I find verse 17 so sobering; God, who usually champions the widow and orphan, says that not even they will receive mercy, for they are as wicked as the rest.

There are many correlations we'd be wise to consider today.

God should be central in our planning process. Don't get me wrong, planning isn't a bad thing – in fact, planning is what often helps us accomplish anything of value. But where do you place God in your planning process? Do you seek Him first and then make your plans? Or make your plans and then ask Him to bless them?

Did you notice the repeated phrase throughout this section? The NIV phrases it as "Yet for all this, His anger is not turned away, His hand is still upraised." It has appeared 5 times so far in the book of Isaiah: 5:25, 9:12, 9:17, 9:21, and 10:4.

Any time a phrase is repeated in Scripture, it's worth taking note.

If I visualize this in my mind, it helps me understand that phrase. For me, it clearly shows impending judgment. The upraised hand makes me think of a parent about to spank a child or someone about to strike down opposition.

Verses 18-21 reminded me that evil is contagious. It spreads like the flu at an elementary school. Beware of thinking you can dabble in it and not be affected. It is an enemy that infiltrates even the strongest of defenses. Our only defense against it is to walk as closely with the Lord as we can, for it's only by the Spirit's power that we can stand against it.

The opening verses of chapter 10 tie in with the end of chapter 9, but shift the focus to injustice. Justice is one of the character traits of God. If we are to be like Him, justice must be a priority for each of us. Often it's the most vulnerable members of society who receive the least justice. How can you take a stand for what's right in the world around you?

This chapter is a call to action – to take a stand against evil and injustice, both privately and publicly. Ask God to show you areas in which you are tolerating evil or injustice and what He might call you to do in response to it.

Isaiah 10:5-34

1. From this chapter, what impresses, stands out, or convicts you?

2. Isaiah 10:5-7
   a. In what ways did Assyria's goals differ from God's plans?

   b. In what areas of your life are you following your own plans rather than trusting God's ways?

3. Isaiah 10:8-19
   a. What do you think is the significance in the mention of the lands and their idols in verses 10-11? What does this reveal about the king's regard for the Lord?

   b. In what areas of your life might you be blinded by pride? For what work of God are you taking or accepting credit?

c. What does verse 15 reveal about the king of Assyria in relation to God? How are people today guilty of this same way of thinking?

d. What might be the significance of the repeated reference to God being a fire or light? Why might this specific image have been meaningful to Isaiah's audience?

4. Isaiah 10:20-27
   a. What specific promises do you find in these verses?

   b. Why do you think God gave Isaiah these two specific past examples in verse 26?

   c. What are some specific examples of God's past faithfulness to you? How could you keep these memories fresh and alive in your mind?

   d. While most of this section deals with what God would do for His people, what were the people to do?

e. Upon whom are you relying? From what burden do you need God's freedom today?

5. Isaiah 10:28-34

a. What do you think is the purpose or main point of these verses?

b. How does the knowledge that God is sovereign over His enemies give you confidence today?

Chapter 10:5-34 – Thoughts and Considerations

Isn't it interesting to contrast God's plans with man's?

The Assyrian king – likely Sennacherib (2 Kings 19:20-37) thought his success and victory was of his own doing. He didn't realize he was little more than a tool God was using to discipline His children.

Did you wonder why God would punish Assyria when they were just doing His work?

The answer lies in these verses. We see in verse 7 that Assyria's goal was total destruction – they were ruthless and violent, seeking to devastate, not discipline. Verses 8 and 12-14 reveal the intense pride, particularly of Sennacherib's heart.

But perhaps worst of all is what we find in verses 9-11. It appears that Sennacherib thinks that God is no better - and, in fact, is inferior – to the idols of the countries he's already conquered.

By this time, Hezekiah had come into power and had abolished much of Judah's idolatry (2 Kings 18:4). If we cross reference this to the historical accounting in Isaiah 37:10-13, we find that the Assyrians not only thought God was inferior, they tried to get the people to doubt God, too. Fortunately, Hezekiah doesn't take the bait and turns to God, but we'll get to that in chapter 37.

Verse 16 specifically talks about a disease. It's quite possible that this refers to the events in Isaiah 37:36 and 2 Kings 19:35 where God struck down much of the Assyrian army overnight. The Bible doesn't specifically say how the army died, but it's possible God sent a wasting, very fast–acting disease to wipe them out. Either way, we see God protecting His people in a glorious and magnificent way.

I thought about the duality of fire as I read verse 17.

Fire is a blessing on a dark or cold night, for it provides heat and light. But it is also difficult to control and can quickly grow, causing catastrophic devastation.

For those of us who know God, He is a blessing and He lights our path (much like He did with a pillar of fire as the nation wandered the desert after the exodus), but He is also a force beyond our control. As believers, we don't have to fear eternal destruction because we are saved by the blood of Jesus, but for any who reject God, God will one day be like a blazing wildfire, leveling all in His path.

His judgment is just, but it is also certain.

God gives the people two very specific examples (verse 26) of times when He had worked powerfully on their behalf – first with the exodus from Egypt and then with the victory at Midian, where God defeated a vast army using an Israelite army of only 300 men (Judges 7).

The result of all this would be that the remnant of Judah would no longer rely upon men, but would rely solely upon the Lord. God goes on to tell them about all the blessings He would give them and the only thing they have to do is rely upon Him. When they chose to do that, their burdens would be lifted and they would grow "fat" – in a good way, signaling abundance.

The chapter ends by showing God's complete and ultimate control over the Assyrian army. It talks about the route they would take, but they would be stopped at Nob, unable to go any further. *God* would hold them back. I think the ultimate message here is that while the Assyrian army is fearsome, God is bigger than all else and will triumph over the enemies of His people.

Isaiah 11

1. From this chapter, what impresses, stands out, or convicts you?

2. Isaiah 11:1-5
   a. What does the imagery in verse 1 (shoot, stump, Branch) reveal to you about the coming Messiah and the nation of Israel?

   b. What do you think it means to delight in the fear of the Lord (v 3, NIV)? How can you put this into practice in your own life today?

   c. Can you think of specific examples where Jesus demonstrated the traits described in verses 2-4?

   d. Which of these traits do you need to ask God to increase in your own life so you can better reflect Christ?

3. Isaiah 11:6-9

    a. What do you think is the significance of the mention of the little child/infant in verses 6 and 8?

    b. What is the reason given for the peace between former enemies?

    c. How might more knowledge of the Lord bring unity and harmony into your own relationships?

4. Isaiah 11:10-16

    a. In what ways have we witnessed a partial fulfillment of verses 10-12 already?

    b. With whom should you be lifting Christ up that He may draw that person to Himself?

    c. What is especially significant to you about verses 13-14?

    d. How do you treat God's people?

e. Toward whom are you harboring hostility or jealousy and how is this damaging to your relationship with that person and your witness for Christ?

f. What point do you think is being made in verses 15-16?

Chapter 11 – Thoughts and Considerations

Isaiah 11 begins with prophecy that most (including me) believe point to Jesus. I love the imagery of the stump and the shoot. A stump is something dead – it's no longer growing or flourishing as a tree, but just sits there until someone rips it from the ground.

In many ways, that's how the worship of God had become in Jesus' day. It was ritual, religion without relationship. We know this because Jesus constantly called the Pharisees out on this very thing.

Yet from that dead thing would come new life – Jesus – who would revolutionize the way people of all time would experience God.

I love how Isaiah, hundreds of years before the coming of Christ, listed out His attributes: bearing fruit, the Spirit of the Lord resting upon Him, wise, understanding, counseling, mighty, knowledgeable, possessing the fear of the Lord, delighting in obeying the Lord, not judging by appearance or hearsay, giving justice, making fair decisions, forceful in word, destroying wickedness, clothed in righteousness and truth.

What a beautiful description! It's fun to read the gospels with this prophecy in mind.

Verse 1 brings up Jesse's son (or David, depending upon your translation). A few fun similarities to consider between David and Jesus – neither was born into royalty, but was chosen by God. Both spent their youth doing ordinary work for their families. They lived in obscurity until God called them forward in His perfect timing.

I was struck by the thought that we likely only know who Jesse is because he was the father of David. Similarly, we know who Mary and Joseph are because they were Jesus' earthly parents. Would we know of any of these individuals if not for their children? I'm not sure we would.

Which brings me to my point – investing in the next generation.

Maybe you're a parent who is struggling through raising your children. Maybe you feel like all your efforts fail. Look to the great parents of the Bible and remember that you never know how God will use your children – and your investment in them – to do mighty works for His Name. Proverbs 22:6 says "Start children off on the way they should go, and even when they are old they will not turn from it." Even if you aren't seeing the fruit now, persevere.

Satan has more influence than he should have in this world because parents don't observe that wise proverb.

And if you aren't a parent, don't think you're off the hook!

There are children all around you – maybe nieces and nephews, cousins, maybe kids at church or your workplace or in your neighborhood – what if you are the only Christian in that child's life? Don't assume someone else will teach them truth. Be God's instrument and tell them about God, about Jesus and the cross, about their need for God and forgiveness through the sacrifice of Jesus.

More than that, *show* them how to live by your example. There may not be anyone else living out Christian principles. We need change in this world and it has to start with someone. Why not you?

I was struck by verse 3 (NIV) that says "He will delight in the fear of the Lord..." You probably already know this, but just in case you don't, I'll say it anyway. Fear, in this instance, is synonymous with reverence or respect, not terror.

If you're like me, you're probably familiar with the idea of fearing the Lord and delighting in the Lord, but delighting in the fear of the Lord was a new concept. I take this to mean that "He" (Jesus) would delight in seeing God honored and revered. His mission would be to point people to the Father and He would rejoice in seeing people turn to God. This is certainly something we see in the gospels as we study the life of Jesus.

Isaiah 11:6 mentions a child leading. I found this passage so rich. Enemies will be at peace and a child – the very image of innocence and vulnerability – would lead. Personally, I believe these verses point to the future when Christ reigns. I can't wait for that day.

I honestly don't know to what time frame the events in verses 10-12 point. There are arguments for the return of the exiles, Christ's first coming, the millennial reign, and even arguments for the church age (in which we're living now). It may point in some ways to all of the above.

If verses 13-16 tie into that same time frame, it would seem to indicate the return from exile, but given that this is prophecy, it may have multiple fulfillments.

The message, however, is clear. God will draw all people to Himself, bringing victory over opposition and blessings beyond compare.

That's something we can all claim through the power of Christ today.

Isaiah 12

1. From this chapter, what impresses, stands out, or convicts you?

2. Do you find any significance in the placement of this chapter in relation to the chapters surrounding it? If so, why do you think this chapter is placed where it is in the book of Isaiah?

3. Isaiah 12:1-3
   a. Do you think Isaiah is referring to a specific comfort in verse 1? If so, what do you think it is?

   b. How has God been a comfort to you when you were deserving of His anger?

   c. How does fear prove a lack of trust in God? What fears do you need to release to God today?

   d. In what ways is God your strength and song?

e. What impact does the image of the well of salvation have on your thinking?

4. Isaiah 12:4-6
   a. For what could the people praise God?

   b. What glorious things has God done in your life lately?

   c. To whom might God be calling you to declare His glorious works this week?

   d. How can you exalt God's name as you go through your daily routines?

5. Isaiah 12:1-6
   a. What patterns and principles for triumphant Christian living do you see modeled in this chapter?

   b. How does your life and your worship of God compare with the model set by these verses? What area do you see as having the greatest opportunity for growth?

Chapter 12 – Thoughts and Considerations

What a beautiful song!

This chapter is all about God and the people's response to His goodness and mercy. It also gives a great model for us to follow in our day-to-day lives.

Personally, I don't think it's coincidental at all that this song of praise erupts right after God promises to send the Messiah, gather His people, and bring peace and security. When we look at who God is and all He's done for us, how can we not respond in thanksgiving and praise?

Our problem is that we too often focus on what seems to be wrong or lacking rather than focusing on the truth of who God is.

Verse 2 talks about trusting God and not being afraid. Fear is the opposite of trust. When we fear, we're really saying that we either think God isn't big enough to handle something or that He isn't loving enough to do what's best – both of which are lies of the enemy, who seeks to disrupt our walk with God and rob us of the assurance given us by God's Spirit.

We see the solution in the very next line.

God is our strength. True, the situation may be bigger than we are. The problem might seem insurmountable, the odds might be too great. Yet God, who holds all things together by His word (Hebrews 1:3), who created the universe by that same word (Psalm 33:6), is more powerful than all that.

The hardest part is releasing the idea that we have any control and trusting in His ultimate control.

I loved the image of the well of salvation in verse 3.

Wells are deep and provide an abundance of life-giving water. We can't see the source of the water, yet when we draw, we are filled with what that source provides.

The same is true of God. He provides us with an abundance of what we need for this life. His resources are deep and vast, beyond our comprehension. We can't see where His Spirit dwells or where He goes, yet we see the results of His Spirit at work in and around us.

Did you notice the way the people's praise overflowed? They didn't just sit quietly and praise God. No! They shouted it to anyone who would listen! In verse 4, they were going to tell the nations of what God had done. In verse 5, they were going to make His praise known around the world.

Good news is meant to be shared.

It's hard. Believe me, I know. I struggle to share it with others in my day to day life. Yet the model we see in Scripture is joyful, abundant sharing that literally bursts from within.

Maybe we just need to get over ourselves enough to live that way.

Isaiah 13

1. From this chapter, what impresses, stands out, or convicts you?

2. Isaiah 13:1-13
   a. What are some of the character traits about this army God has assembled?

   b. Do you think this passage refers to a human army fighting a physical battle, a spiritual army fighting a spiritual battle, or both? Why?

   c. Do you think this passage is referring only to Babylon's destruction? Why or why not?

   d. What do you think is the message of verses 7-8?

   e. What specific sins are mentioned in this passage? Think about how some of these sins may have infiltrated your own life – what changes do you need to make?

f. What would be some of the consequences of these sins?

3. Isaiah 13:14-22
   a. What will be the fate of Babylon and its inhabitants?

   b. From all you have learned so far, what correlations do you see between Babylon and our country?

   c. What must our nation do to avoid the same fate as Babylon?

   d. What is the role of the church in implementing these changes?

   e. What adjustments to your own life might God be calling you to make to be a part of this process?

Chapter 13 – Thoughts and Considerations

Chapter 13 marks a turning point in our study. We're entering the chapters on judgment – first on pagan nations, but then also on Israel and Judah.

Judgment can be really hard to look at but it's a necessary part of justice. We'll look at this in depth in the next eleven chapters. If you find yourself lagging as you go through these chapters, look for the messages of hope and mercy that shine through, for God is both just and merciful.

We see that God Himself has assembled this army to do the work set before them. Even in times of trouble and despair, know that nothing is beyond God's control.

He doesn't stand there, wringing His hands, wishing He could do something. Not even close.

He can alter events at any time in countless ways so that His will is accomplished. We may not understand why He doesn't intervene in bad situations, but part of faith is believing He knows what is best, even when things are at the absolute darkest.

The chapter opens by saying this is about the destruction of Babylon, but many of these events seem much larger than the demise of an empire – even one as powerful and massive as Babylon. The destruction of all sinners, the darkening of the heavens, and the shaking of the earth (vs 9-13) feel more like what you'd read in Joel or Revelation, which address end times. Now, Scripture clearly tells us this prophecy is for Babylon, so it obviously describes what will happen to Babylon, but I'm going with my standard train of thought that this prophecy has multiple fulfillments with larger and further reaching implications than simply the destruction of Babylon.

It's interesting how in verse 14 Isaiah specifically says that the

Babylonians will be like sheep without a shepherd. Jesus is the good Shepherd and those of us who follow Him are His sheep. He protects, shelters, and sacrifices for us. Yet the Babylonians didn't know the one true God, so they truly were Shepherd-less sheep.

Verse 17 foretells the fall of Babylon to the Medes... which is precisely what happened. The Medo-Persian Empire, led by Cyrus the great, destroyed Babylon, just as God declared.

It's especially interesting to note that Babylon would only be inhabited by wild animals.

I think the animals listed have special significance. Jackals, for instance, are almost always mentioned in a negative light in the Bible. Jackals and Hyenas are both scavengers and, according to Leviticus 11:26-28, contact with dead bodies made people unclean – I would assume that since these animals scavenge dead things, they would, by extension, also be unclean. Owls are included in the list of unclean animals given in Leviticus 11:13-18. This alone would have gotten the attention of Isaiah's original audience.

Our culture likes to make a mockery of divine judgment.

Think about the last time you heard someone talk about God tossing lightning bolts to smite the wicked. Perhaps we make light of it to avoid the seriousness of the topic. It makes us uncomfortable, doesn't it? We'd much rather focus on God's love and mercy.

Yet mercy cannot exist without justice. If there's no judgment, there's no room for mercy. They are the balances at either end of the scale. They are also two distinct facets of God's character.

I think the key in this passage is verse 11. God's wrath will come on the wicked, the haughty, and the ruthless.

That's why we so desperately need a Savior, for without Jesus, we are all those things. But because of Jesus' death and resurrection, we can be clothed in Jesus through faith (Romans 13:14, Galatians 3:26-27) so that when God sees us, He sees Christ. Not that we're always great at reflecting Him, but God chooses to view us in light of Jesus' sacrifice for us.

So while it's tough to look at judgment, that judgment should cause us to run to the only One who can save us from it.

Isaiah 14

1. From this chapter, what impresses, stands out, or convicts you?

2. Isaiah 14:1-3
   a. How would God demonstrate His compassion to His persecuted people?

   b. What are some evidences of God's compassion in your own life?

3. Isaiah 14:4-11
   a. In what ways had the Babylonian king brought the judgment upon Himself?

   b. How does this passage give you hope when you consider some of the atrocities committed by wicked leaders today?

   c. What warning can you take from God's judgment against this king?

4. Isaiah 14:12-21

    a. Depending on your translation, this passage may state it refers to the Babylonian king or Lucifer. What correlations do you see between the two?

    b. What root sin motivated the king/Lucifer to act as he did?

    c. What contrasts do you see between what the king/Lucifer strove to achieve and what actually awaited him?

    d. In what areas are you exalting yourself?

5. Isaiah 14:22-32

    a. What burdens do leaders or governments place upon people today?

    b. In what ways might you be guilty of oppressing another, whether actively or passively?

    c. Toward whom does God show special concern in these verses? In what ways might He be calling you to do the same?

Chapter 14 – Thoughts and Considerations

This chapter opens with God tenderly promising to take care of His people. Judgment is necessary, but God still loves His sinful, rebellious people.

The fate of the Babylonian king is not so pleasant. This proud, wicked king who oppressed people with relentless violence is promised a home among the dead. Verse 11 hits the root cause of the king's demise – pride.

Scripture doesn't specifically identify him, but I don't think his identity is what's important here. What matters are the lessons we can learn from him. As we continue on in this study, you'll see how often God condemns pride. Pride causes us to set ourselves up in God's place. God says He opposes the proud, but gives grace to the humble (James 4:6). Where is pride creeping into your life?

The other thing that stands out to me from this section is that God cares about how we treat others. It's easy to read these verses and think that we aren't like this, but there are many ways we can persecute or oppress other people. Sometimes it's the things we say or the way we say them. Passing judgment on others can also be a form of oppression. Sometimes – and I think this one is a sneaky one – we persecute or oppress people by NOT taking action when we should.

Passivity is one of the great evils of our current age.

As Christians, we're called to be Christ-like. Jesus actively opposed injustice and oppression. How can you take a stand today?

Verse 12 starts a section that can be a little confusing and is translated differently depending upon which version you're reading. I don't claim to have all the answers. Tradition holds that these verses refer to Lucifer's fall. It certainly seems to be speaking of someone much larger and grander than a single Babylonian king.

It's possible that it refers to both Lucifer and a king. Certainly some parts don't seem to work for a mere king, just like other parts don't seem to fit for Lucifer.

Regardless of the meaning, there is a strong warning here. The man (Lucifer/king) attempted to set himself up in God's place. Verse 14 shows an intentional self-exaltation with the goal of surpassing God's power and greatness.

Yet God will share His glory with no one else (Isaiah 42:8, 48:11).

Judgment will come and it will be irrevocable. Once again, we see the steep price of pride.

Did you notice that God is the one who is acting (vs 22-27)? Sure, He's using people to do His work, but at the core, He is the one coming against His enemies. He will act on behalf of the burdened and no one can stop Him.

The chapter closes with a warning to the Philistines about rejoicing at the trouble of others. No matter what they've done, we should never rejoice at the suffering of other people. The only reason we don't receive a similar fate is because of God's mercy and compassion.

I love how God shows special care for the poor and needy (v 30), as well as the humble (v 32). Even in these passages of judgment, God's mercy shines through. God establishes a safe haven for His people and provides a refuge we won't find anywhere else.

Isaiah 15-16

1. From these chapters, what impresses, stands out, or convicts you?

2. Isaiah 15:1-9
   a. To whom did the Moabites turn in their distress?

   b. Judging by the rest of chapter 15, did their "helper" provide any relief?

   c. To what or whom do you look for help?

   d. What are some of the things in which the Moabites placed their trust?

   e. In what ways might you be looking to another person, wealth, status, or possessions for security?

   f. What warnings do you see in verse 9?

3. Isaiah 16:1-5

   a. To whom does it appear Moab would turn for shelter?

   b. Given their situation and other options, do you think this was wise? Why or why not?

   c. Who is your most trusted human advisor? From whom does this person draw their knowledge?

   d. How would this promise be a tremendous comfort to the people in their current circumstances?

   e. Do you think verse 5 refers to Jesus or simply to a good king established and led by God? Why?

   f. Who is on the throne of your heart? What in your life gives evidence to your answer?

4. Isaiah 16:6-8

   a. What results did Moab's pride bring upon the land?

b. In what ways do you see this happening in our own country?

c. Where has pride taken root in your life?

5. Isaiah 16:9-14

a. Previously in 15:5, and here again, the narrator mourns with Moab. Do you think this mourning is from Isaiah or God? Why?

b. What do you learn about the proper response to the distress of others from these verses? To whom might God be calling you to reach out in compassion or support during a trial?

c. What do you think is the significance of the frequent mentioning of agricultural losses?

d. What does God reveal about the sources of Moab's hope in verse 12?

e. What results when we place our trust in the false or temporal?

f. Why do you think God gave such a specific timeframe for this prophecy when most prophecies lack this level of detail?

g. What do your actions reveal about how seriously you take God and His words?

Chapters 15~16 ~ Thoughts and Considerations

As we consider the next few chapters and look at the judgment upon the nations, you might want to find a map of Biblical times and see the landscape. It can really help establish a sense of setting and make the promises of these passages come alive. I found a map online that showed a lot of the ancient cities referenced in these chapters and if you take a few minutes to do a search, you'll likely find some good options, too.

We look at these chapters together because they truly go together. Both deal with the destruction that would come upon Moab.

Moab descended from the incestuous relationship between Lot and his oldest daughter following the destruction of Sodom and Gomorrah (Genesis 19:37). It's even possible that Sodom and Gomorrah were located in the land that Moab would come to occupy (compare Genesis 13:10-13 with Genesis 19:23-38). We learn from Genesis 13 that it was fertile, good land – which is why Lot chose it for himself. The chief god of the Moabites was Chemosh and the Moabites drew the Israelites into idolatry on at least one occasion (Numbers 25:1-3).

We see the judgment on Moab would be swift and thorough. Ar and Kir would be destroyed in a single night. Remember that these people didn't have bombs, so the destruction of an entire city in a single night is quite a feat.

There would be great mourning throughout the land. The people would turn to their gods for help, but their gods cannot help them.

How sad that they wouldn't turn to the one, true God for help. If they had, perhaps their fate might have been different.

They would flee with their wealth, but destruction would

follow them still. There is no escaping from Almighty God. I'm assuming the lion referenced in 15:9 is figurative and that the real instrument of destruction would be an enemy army, but it's hard to say.

Either way, Scripture makes it clear that justice can't be avoided.

16:1 talks about sending lambs to the ruler of the land. An interesting correlation to this is that Moab did this very thing after David defeated them (2 Samuel 8:2) and it appears that they continued paying tribute to David until the Moabite rebellion in 2 Kings 3:4-5. In light of this, it's possible that Isaiah 16:1 indicates that Moab might once again pay tribute to Judah in an attempt to earn Judah's favor and secure Judah's help.

While they should be seeking God's help, I'm thinking this might indicate that they at least recognized that there was something different about Judah's God. Maybe I'm stretching in this, but Judah doesn't seem like they'd be an obvious ally – it was a small nation compared to others (like Egypt) and lacked the resources and military might that Egypt possessed.

Chapter 16 starts with the mention of refugees seeking help. Just like we aren't to revel in the misery of others, we should also offer assistance as we're able, especially to those who are particularly weak or vulnerable.

I love this promise of the good king! Personally, I again suspect a dual fulfillment – possibly in a good earthly king like Hezekiah, but ultimately fulfilled by Jesus. He alone is the only one who can truly rule faithfully, with perfect justice and righteousness.

Once again, in verse 6 we see that the wrath poured out upon Moab is a result of pride (arrogance and boasting are effects of pride).

What really struck me, though, is the response to the devastation of Moab. Isaiah 15:5 and 16:9-11 shows an "I" character – presumably Isaiah, although it could refer to God (idea supported by the ending of verse 10) – weeping for Moab. The people's idolatry and blatant rebellion had brought the judgment down upon their heads, yet there is no joy in their troubles.

We would be wise to follow this example.

How do you respond when you witness the trouble of others, particularly those who have been unkind or spiteful to you? Do you smugly think that they're getting what they deserve? Or does your heart break for them?

The chapter concludes with a very definitive timeline.

It's not often that you see this kind of detail in the prophets, yet for some reason God gives it here. Maybe it was to give credence to Isaiah's prophecies in the eyes of the people. It might've also been so Moab would know they only had a limited amount of time to repent. The final sentence of this chapter reveals God's mercy and hope for the future.

The wrath awaiting Moab would not completely wipe the Moabites out. Though they would be few, there would be survivors.

Isaiah 17

1. From this chapter, what impresses, stands out, or convicts you?

2. Isaiah 17:1-8
   a. What might be meant by the references to Israel's former glory?

   b. What hope is offered in verse 6?

   c. Prior to "that day" (v 7), what do you think the people looked to or relied upon?

   d. How do you see this happening in our country today? How do you see it happening in our churches?

   e. In what current trial are you failing to put your trust in God alone?

3. Isaiah 17:9-11

    a. In what situations – past or present – has God proven Himself to be your rock and refuge?

    b. How do these verses illustrate the futility of man's efforts compared to God's power?

    c. What are you presently attempting to accomplish in your own strength?

4. Isaiah 17:12-14

    a. To what nations or people do you think these verse refer?

    b. What does this comparison to roaring waters and raging seas tell you about the nations?

    c. What are some ways that people – even Christians – loot or plunder God's people/the church today?

Chapter 17 – Thoughts and Considerations

Damascus was the capital of Syria/Aram, therefore it's logical to assume that the fall of Damascus symbolizes the fall of the entire nation. Similarly, the judgments upon Damascus may actually be judgments upon the entire nation.

Syria/Aram and Israel actually formed an alliance (2 Kings 16:5) with a goal of conquering Jerusalem. They failed, but it's possible that this is the reason the two nations are tied together in this passage.

Another theory is that perhaps Isaiah delivered this message around the same timeframe. Interestingly enough, the attack by Syria/Aram and Israel is what sent King Ahaz running to the king of Assyria for help – we studied this back in chapter 7 when Isaiah warned Ahaz not to align with Assyria.

We see yet again that God promises to preserve a remnant (v 6) – a common theme throughout the passages of judgment. Did you notice that verse 6 doesn't say that it would be the most righteous "olives" preserved? It just says that there would be some remaining.

That's mercy.

None of us deserve God's provision, protection, or favor. He just gives it to us anyway, regardless of who we are or what we've done.

God's justice would have the desired effect. The people would turn from their worthless idolatry and would look to God alone. I like the finality of verses 7-8. The way it's worded makes it sound as though this would be a permanent change, that the people would never again turn to idols. I'm not sure that this is truly what the text is saying, but what a glorious thing it would be!

The admonition in verses 9-10 is so applicable to us today.

The wording in verses 8-9 leads me to believe that these are the things in which the people previously put their hopes: idols and the works of their hands.

It honestly reminds me a lot of our culture today. We're taught to be self-sufficient, to rely on family or friends, or to rely on the government. None of these things is necessarily bad in and of itself, except that we often rely upon those things more than God.

The truly sad thing is that we can see those attitudes infiltrate the church, too. Often the church relies upon attendance numbers, programs, specific ministries, or traditions rather than relying fully upon God.

We can see what happens when we rely upon anyone or anything other than God.

Verses 10-11 show that God's will prevails, despite man's plans or best efforts. God has given us all abilities and gifts to use in His power and for His glory, but when we try to take off and do things in our own strength, our efforts will not amount to much.

Verses 12-14 show the fate of all who oppose God's people. They may be mighty and powerful, but just as a wave breaks on the beach and slides back to the sea, so those who oppose God will lose their power and fall.

This is good news for all of us who belong to God. It brings to mind Romans 8:31: "...If God is for us, who can be against us?"

Isaiah 18

1. From this chapter, what impresses, stands out, or convicts you?

2. Isaiah 18:1-7
   a. Compare the description of the Cushites/Ethiopians (v 2) with the description of God (v 4). How does the contrast between these descriptions impact you?

   b. What do these verses tell you about the way the Cushites/Ethiopians were viewed by other nations?

   c. What might be the message behind verse 3? Why do you think it was placed between the messages before and after it?

   d. What significance do you see in the Lord's words in verse 4?

   e. How do you respond when it feels like God is passively watching in times of trouble?

f. In what current struggle do you need to rest in God's faithful, yet sometimes unassuming, presence?

g. What do you see as the main point of verses 5-6?

h. According to verse 7, how will the events described change the Cushites/Ethiopians?

i. Who are the "Cushites/Ethiopians" in your own life?

j. When has God used circumstances beyond your control to draw you back to Himself or teach you to rely upon Him?

Chapter 18 – Thoughts and Considerations

Cush – or Ethiopia or Sudan, depending upon your translation – is a bit of a mystery to us. Given the topography of the area and the frequent references to water here, it seems likely that it would be somewhere around the Nile River or one of its tributaries. It's believed to have been a land of great wealth, something that is hinted at in Job 28:19.

Whoever these people were, there are a few things we can glean from this chapter in Isaiah. They were tall and smooth-skinned people who were mighty warriors and widely feared (v 2, 7), and who used the rivers as a means of transportation (v 2).

The contrast between these people and God is quite startling. The people are portrayed as fierce and ruthless, causing the nations to tremble, yet in verse 4 we see God watching quietly.

Was God worried about these people and their plans?

Hardly. Verses 5-6 show that God would thwart their plans and ultimately bring them to Himself (v 7).

I'm not sure if the gifts they bring in verse 7 are voluntary because they want to honor God or forced because they have been conquered and must pay tribute, but either way, they would come under God's control.

So while the nations were afraid of the Cushites because of their perceived power, God is the One who ultimately had true power.

Do you ever feel like God is passively observing your troubles? These verses should be a huge encouragement! God sees all your troubles and will take action in His time. More than that, no matter how big the trouble seems to you, God is not worried. He holds all things in His mighty hand.

There are a lot of Cushites in our lives today. They might come in the form of financial woes, trouble in the workplace, stresses at home, strained relationships with family, violence, legal troubles, or any number of other things, but the important thing to notice is that all earthly troubles and powers are fleeting. These things will one day fade away and God will remain.

So choose today to focus on Him. Let Him have your worries, your stresses, and your troubles. He can handle them all.

Isaiah 19

1. From this chapter, what impresses, stands out, or convicts you?

2. Isaiah 19:1-4
   a. What might be the reason Isaiah mentions Egypt's idols before addressing the Egyptian people themselves?

   b. To whom would the Egyptians turn in their distress? How did this make them vulnerable to subjection under a cruel master?

   c. To whom does our society say we should turn with our troubles? In what situations are you currently buying into this lie?

3. Isaiah 19:5-10
   a. Why would this threat against the Nile be particularly devastating to the Egyptians?

   b. How could these verses also be taken symbolically to describe the condition of their souls?

c. What droughts do you see in our culture today? How are they evident in our churches? In your own life?

4. Isaiah 19:11-17
   a. What would be the test to distinguish whether the wise men were truly wise?

   b. What are some things that our society calls wise? How do these things line up with the truth in God's word?

   c. Do the people to whom you look for leadership or advice draw their wisdom and strength from God? How can you tell?

5. Isaiah 19:18-25
   a. What is especially significant to you from the prophecies contained in these verses?

   b. What offerings might God be asking you to bring to Him today?

   c. What do you learn from the prophecy in verses 23-25? What does this tell you about God?

Chapter 19 – Thoughts and Considerations

There's a lot of remarkable things in this chapter. Egypt, long an enemy of Israel, would not escape God's just wrath.

One of the first things that stood out to me was that the idols are mentioned before the Egyptian people (v 1). I wonder if this is to highlight the extreme superiority of God to these impotent idols. The sight of God advancing against the country would make the idols – in whom the Egyptian people were placing their trust – tremble in fear.

Still, we see that the Egyptians don't see the true state of their idols, for again in verse 3, they are turning to the idols for help. In addition, they would turn to spirits and mediums for help. But what good is consulting the *dead* on matters of life?

Before you shake your head at them for their foolishness, let's pause and think. There are so many things we do today that really are no different.

How do we respond when trouble comes?

We turn to friends and family, to the government, to the rich or powerful... or ourselves... to try to find relief from our struggles. Too often, we attempt to apply only human logic. We make God our last resort instead of our first choice.

Now none of the things I mentioned above are bad options; but if we haven't gone to God first and used those options following His leading, then we're no wiser than the Egyptians.

The Nile is the life source of Egypt. It would flood at given times each year, depositing nutrients in the soil and leaving those nutrients behind when the waters receded. If the Nile dried up, it would have brought catastrophic drought and famine to the land.

What's truly interesting is the way this drought mirrored the souls of the Egyptian people. Without God, their souls were dry and parched, stinking and lined with rot.

We see the same or similar droughts in our nation today. Our country is polluted with "churches" that don't teach truth, that pick and choose what to believe from the Bible and what to leave out, that are more concerned with political correctness and popular opinion than with what God has to say.

Don't get me wrong, we're to speak the truth in love (Ephesians 4:15), but we are still to speak the truth, even when people don't like what the truth has to say.

Look at Jesus. Did He ever cower instead of speaking the hard messages? No! He always spoke the truth, even when it put His life in danger. Don't believe me? Check out John 8 (among countless others).

We see Isaiah practicing this same principle. Do you think people wanted to hear the messages he was saying? I doubt it. The message of verse 11 is hardly sensitive or tolerant.

Yet, it's the truth God gave him and he spoke it faithfully.

In spite of the hard truth, there's hope. In verses 18-25, we see the Egyptian people turning to the Lord. Verse 18 is significant because the city referenced there (city of destruction in some translations, city of the sun or Heliopolis in others) was the center of worship for Egypt's sun god Ra. Because of this, the city would have been steeped in idolatry.

Yet here, we see the people of that city turning from their nonexistent god to the one true God.

It's amazing that both the Egyptians and Assyrians would worship God alongside Israel. This is a picture of the work God does through His true church today. He brings together people of all cultures, all nations, all backgrounds, and unites them in Himself. People who were formerly enemies can find unity and peace when they fix their eyes upon the Savior.

I love the way this chapter closes. God speaks highly personal blessings on these groups of people. He calls Egypt "My people," Assyria "the land I have made," and Israel "My special possession."

To all of us who belong to Jesus, God says the same thing today. 1 Peter 2:9 – "But you are a chosen people, a royal priesthood, a holy nation, God's special possession, that you may declare the praises of Him who called you out of darkness into His wonderful light."

Isaiah 20

1. From this chapter, what impresses, stands out, or convicts you?

2. Isaiah 20:1-4
   a. What trials and challenges might Isaiah have experienced during those 3 years?

   b. Do you think Isaiah proclaimed a message during that time or was his odd behavior the message?

   c. What are some instances where God might call you to be silent and let your life declare His truth?

   d. Why do you think Egypt is singled out at the end of verse 4 ("to Egypt's shame")?

   e. Why do you think God would ask Isaiah, His faithful servant, to do something so humiliating?

    f. Can you think of a time when you suffered humiliation or disgrace for Christ's sake?

3. Isaiah 20:5-6
    a. How do these verses prove God's ultimate point about the futility in trusting man?

    b. In times of crisis, do you turn to God first or only when your plans have failed? How can you change this to make God your first choice every time?

Chapter 20 – Thoughts and Considerations

This is one of those rare, isolated chapters where we get a brief glimpse of Isaiah's life.

Being a prophet wasn't a fun job; at times, God called His prophets to do very strange things as a sign to the people. Ezekiel, especially, records some seemingly odd behaviors, yet – like Isaiah – he was obedient to God's call.

Ashdod was a Philistine city. From 1 Samuel 5:1-8, we find that there was a temple to Dagon, a Philistine god, in Ashdod. Ashdod briefly housed the Ark of the Covenant after the Philistines captured it in battle.

The year that Ashdod fell to the Assyrians, God calls Isaiah to do what most of us would deem unthinkable – walk around stripped and barefoot.

Can you imagine being Isaiah during these three years?

The ridicule and shame he must have faced! However, he chose to be obedient to God, in spite of the discomfort and embarrassment that obedience caused.

It's a good lesson to us.

God often calls us out of our comfort zones. Obedience can be uncomfortable at best. Sometimes obedience can cost us dearly. Yet there's a peace about being in God's will, no matter our circumstances.

I find it interesting that there's no mention of a message here.

It doesn't mean Isaiah didn't prophesy during those three years, however in this instance, it appears his actions themselves would serve as the sign (v 3). Often, God calls us to declare His truth verbally, but there are instances where we're to be silent and let our actions speak for us. The trick is discerning between the two and following through with what God calls you to do.

In times of war, it wasn't uncommon for conquered peoples to be forced into slavery and led away naked and chained. God promises this will be the fate of Egypt and Ethiopia, evidently the nations in whom the Philistines had put their trust.

Once again, we see the futility of placing our trust in anything or anyone but God. Nations fall, people fail, plans come undone, but God is never stopped, surprised, or thwarted.

As in previous chapters, we are admonished to put our trust in God first. God will never let us down. In fact, Scripture tells us that those who trust in the Lord will never be put to shame (Psalm 25:3).

True, Isaiah likely experienced shame and humiliation during those three years, but God must have sustained him for him to persevere through it. And now, as Isaiah dwells with God for all eternity, he likely has forgotten all about those three years, for his reward is in God.

So if God has called you to a difficult, uncomfortable, or painful task, follow Isaiah's example and press on. God has a plan for you in it and your obedience will bring God's blessing and eternal rewards.

Isaiah 21

1. From this chapter, what impresses, stands out, or convicts you?

2. Isaiah 21:1-5
   a. Why might Isaiah have addressed this to the "desert by the sea" in verse 1 rather than clearly stating Babylon as he does in verse 9?

   b. What do verses 1-2 reveal about this impending attack?

   c. Assuming Isaiah is speaking of himself in verses 3-4, what do you learn about the impact his visions had upon him?

   d. How sensitive are you to the suffering of others? To whom can you show compassion today?

3. Isaiah 21:6-10
   a. What parallels do you see between the lookout/watchman and Isaiah himself?

b. In what present situation has God made you a watchman? What message has He given you to declare?

4. Isaiah 21:11-12
   a. What messages or warnings do you see in this short oracle?

5. Isaiah 21:13-17
   a. What call did God place upon the people of Arabia?

   b. What "war-ravaged fugitives" exist in your sphere of influence and how might God be calling you to help them?

   c. What significance do you see in the way Isaiah ends this passage – "The LORD, the God of Israel, has spoken"?

Chapter 21 – Thoughts and Considerations

I find it interesting that Isaiah doesn't clearly identify the country (later identified as Babylon in verse 9), yet calls it the desert by the sea. Perhaps it signifies the state of the souls of the people there – dry and barren, parched, and devoid of life.

Whatever the reason for the wording he chose, the fate of the nation is clear. The attack would be swift, there would be mass destruction, and there would be betrayal.

I would assume Isaiah is speaking of himself in verses 3-4 and wonder about the depth of the visions he received. It almost seems like he lived them – at least to some degree – like a very vivid dream that feels so real it leaves you upset, even after awaking. Can you imagine "living" the destruction and devastation of all the nations as Isaiah might have?

I love the illustration of a watchman.

A watchman's job was very simple, but critically important. He was to keep watch, typically from the top of the walls surrounding a city or from some other elevated location that would allow him to see any who approached – sounding an alarm if those approaching were dangerous or announcing the visitor, especially if it was royalty.

God specifically calls Ezekiel a watchman (Ezekiel 33:7), but all prophets were essentially watchmen. Their "job" was to look out for the people, warn of danger (typically unchecked sin and idolatry), and announce and declare God.

We, too, are watchmen.

If you are a follower of Christ, there are people in your life whom God has charged you with "watching over." It might be a child or family member. It could be friends or neighbors, people at church, or people in your workplace. We all have a call to point people to God and declare truth. How seriously do you take that responsibility?

Verses 11-12 are a bit of a mystery to me. It sounded to me like the watchman was warning that the danger had momentarily passed, but would return again, that there would be no true peace or respite from their struggles.

It could also contain a warning to be vigilant as the watchman encourages the one asking the questions to "come back yet again."

Complacency is a trap that is so easy to fall into, yet can be deadly once we are there. Think what would have happened if the people in Jerusalem grew complacent because they weren't under attack. It would have made them very easy to invade and conquer.

Or what about the watchman? If he'd thought there was no danger and then chose to take a nap, utter devastation could have befallen the city.

The same is true for us spiritually.

Those sins you think you've conquered, or areas where you think you would never fall, might just be the sins that trip you up in the future. We must constantly be on guard against the attacks of the enemy. A close walk with the Lord is our surest line of defense against complacency and sin.

The chapter ends with what appears to be a charge to Arabia to care for the refugees from the war-ravaged countries. We see once again that God cares about the individual. He often chooses to use people to do His good work in caring for others.

There are war-ravaged refugees all around us. You don't even have to look far to find the needs. People who need help financially, the homeless, the elderly, shut-ins, foster kids, the lonely, the abused, the imprisoned. Needs are everywhere; where might God be leading you to get involved? If you're not sure where to start, just ask a pastor – you'll wind up with a list longer than you might imagine!

God closes this chapter by announcing who has spoken – the Lord, the God of Israel. I see it almost as a signature. God has declared all that will happen, and in case there are any doubts, He seals it with His Name.

Isaiah 22

1. From this chapter, what impresses, stands out, or convicts you?

2. Isaiah 22:1-4
   a. In what ways do the people's and leaders' actions show their lack of trust in God?

   b. What recent situation in your life have you – or are you – viewing with the eyes of the world rather than the eyes of faith?

3. Isaiah 22:5-11
   a. How did the people respond to this invasion? What emotions or attitudes do you see as the motivators of their response?

   b. Do you think the actions the people took to protect themselves in verses 9-11 were wrong? Why or why not? What fatal mistake did the people make?

    c. How do you see this pattern repeated in our country and churches today?

    d. In what current struggle are you striving in your own strength, seeking to fulfill your plans rather than God's will?

4. Isaiah 22:12-14

    a. Why did God call the people to mourn? What do the people's words reveal about their attitudes?

    b. Why do you think God would not accept any atonement for the peoples' sins?

5. Isaiah 22:15-25

    a. Why would this disaster come upon Shebna? What sins motivated his actions?

    b. What does Eliakim reveal about the nature of a true servant of God?

c. To whom do you think verse 25 refers? Why do you think this fate would befall the peg?

d. In what situation are you revealing the self-centeredness of Shebna rather than the integrity of Eliakim?

Chapter 22 – Thoughts and Considerations

This sobering chapter has a lot of warnings for us today – warnings against self-reliance, self-exaltation, and taking the words of the Lord lightly.

Verse 1 mentions running to the rooftops; there are several possibilities as to what this might mean. It could mean that they were looking for a good vantage point to see what was going on, or perhaps they thought the rooftops were safer and carried lower risk of discovery. It's also possible that this ties in to pagan rituals, as it wasn't uncommon for incense to be burned to false gods from the rooftops.

Whatever it means, there's one thing we clearly do not see in these first few verses – the people on their knees seeking the Lord's help. Disaster is coming and they scurry around to escape it – not that I'm judging because I'd probably be right there with them – but what they should have done first was pray.

If you're reading the NIV, verse 3 indicates that they were surrendering and fleeing while the enemy was still far away (some other translations omit this), showing their complete lack of faith in God. The battle hadn't even reached their doorstep and they've already given up. There are so many times in Israel's history where God fought the battle for His people, yet these people were quick to forget.

That's why it's so important to dwell on God's past faithfulness to us. It increases our faith and reminds us of his presence during the hard times.

The battle reaches Jerusalem's gates. The Assyrian army is vast, having conquered many other nations (likely why verse 6 references people from Elam and Kir joining in the attack). Those left in Jerusalem fight... in their own strength. They gather weapons and try to repair the walls.

Yet in verse 11, we see that they ignore their most valuable resource and don't use their greatest weapon – "But you never ask for help from the One who did all this. You never considered the One who planned this long ago."

Would the outcome have been different had they repented and sought the Lord? We'll never know, for they didn't choose that wise option.

In fact, they went the opposite way.

Verse 12 shows that God called them to repent, however in verse 13 we see them having a grand party. "Let's feast and drink, for tomorrow we die!" could be taken as a mockery of Isaiah's (and all the prophets') warnings, or it may have reflected a "here and now" attitude toward life.

Do either of those sound like attitudes we commonly see portrayed today?

I'm especially struck by the "here and now" lifestyle. Our society – and, if we're honest, we can probably clump ourselves into that category – sells the idea of living for today, of focusing only on what you want at any given moment in time and not focusing on the future at all.

This is really a two-edged sword.

On the one hand, we shouldn't spend so much time focusing on and planning for the future that we fail to seize the opportunities provided to us today, especially in regard to sharing the gospel or investing in the relationships in our lives, because we have not been promised tomorrow. God might call you home today.

On the other hand, if we live only for the here and now with no thought about the future, we'll find that the works of our hands and the fruit of our lives amounts to very little in the scheme of eternity.

So how do we balance the two? I think it's our focus. Are we focused on self-pleasure and self-fulfillment or are we focused on pleasing God and ministering to others?

The chapter ends with this interesting section focusing on two very different individuals: Shebna and Eliakim. In ancient times, burial was a very important topic. To be left unburied was a disgrace. Here, we see Shebna, the palace administrator, preparing a grand (and likely expensive) tomb for himself. I wonder if it wasn't at the expense of his master, if he wasn't abusing his power and position – verse 18 ends with the phrase "you are a disgrace to your master."

Planning the details of end of life isn't a bad thing, but again, it's the attitude with which he was approaching this. He was seeking glory and honor for himself. I see the root sins of this being pride and self-exaltation.

Isaiah's prophecy is completely fulfilled. Interestingly enough, if not for this passage, we likely wouldn't have ever known that Shebna at one time held the administrator position. We find references to Shebna in 2 Kings 18-19 and Isaiah 36-37, both of which refer to him simply as the secretary.

The language used to refer to Eliakim's service while in the administrator position is very interesting. In fact, verse 22 closely mirrors Jesus' words in Matthew 16:19 and the wording in Revelation 3:7. Honestly, I don't know what it all means, but it sounds as though God would reward his faithfulness with divine authority. It's also possible that Eliakim, in some ways, is symbolic of Jesus, for many of these phrases are applicable to the Messiah as well.

Verse 25 speaks of God removing the peg (or nail) and everything crashing down when it is removed.

Again, I'm not too sure what it all means. I did come up with a few possibilities, though I'm sure there are many others and I might be wrong on all counts.

It could refer simply to Eliakim. Perhaps the burdens of his position became too much to bear and he made a mistake that caused the nation to suffer. It could refer to the fall of Jerusalem, with Jerusalem being the nail or peg and when it fell, the whole nation also fell. It could also refer to Jesus' death. When Jesus died on the cross, the entire religious system to which the people had grown accustomed – the temple worship and sacrifices – came crashing down. They were no longer needed for Jesus had taken the place and perfectly fulfilled the law.

No matter what it means, we can see one thing quite clearly. God was perfectly in control of things. He knew what the peg represented, He knew what would happen when it was removed, and He removed it in His perfect timing. We can trust God in all circumstances because He is never surprised by the events that occur. He already knows what will happen and is sovereign over the outcome.

Isaiah 23

1. From this chapter, what impresses, stands out, or convicts you?

2. Isaiah 23:1-14
   a. What do you learn about Tyre from these verses?

   b. What do you think is the primary message of verse 4?

   c. Of what was Tyre proud?

   d. What current trial might God be using to humble you?

   e. Why did God draw their attention to the fate of the Babylonians?

   f. What examples has God placed before you as a warning?

g. Note the specific things that will be destroyed or taken away: house and harbor (1, 10), and fortresses (11, 14). Why do you think these things were specifically mentioned?

h. In what false securities are you placing your trust?

3. Isaiah 23:15-18
   a. Why might Tyre be compared to a prostitute?

   b. Do you think Tyre will serve God? If so, why would Isaiah say Tyre would return to her hire as a prostitute? If not, why might her profits be set apart for the Lord?

Chapter 23 – Thoughts and Considerations

Tyre is one of those nations that crops up repeatedly throughout Israel's history. They provided wood and laborers to help build King David's palace (2 Samuel 5:11, 1 Chronicles 14:1). They later helped Solomon build the temple by again providing wood and at least one skilled laborer (1 Kings 5:7, 2 Chronicles 2). In return, Solomon gave them wheat, barley, olive oil, and wine (1 Kings 5:11, 2 Chronicles 2:15). Ezra records that Tyre provided materials in the temple's rebuilding following the return from exile. Additionally, Jesus may have spent time in Tyre (Matthew 15:21, Mark 7:24).

Their influence wasn't always good, however.

For example, in Amos 1:9-10, it's recorded that Tyre disregarded a treaty and sold slaves to Edom. The victims aren't named, however the judgment implies that they may have been God's people. Sidon was the mother city of Tyre and Sidon oppressed the Israelites (Judges 10:12). Additionally, Jezebel, arguably the vilest, most wicked queen in Scripture, came from Sidon (1 Kings 16:31-33).

From these verses, we can ascertain that Tyre was a successful port city, one relied upon by other nations for business success. The destruction of Tyre would have likely had a ripple effect on the other nations. Egypt specifically is mentioned here, yet I doubt Egypt mourned for Tyre; more likely they mourned the financial loss Tyre's destruction brought on them.

The things God specifically mentions that He will remove – house, harbor, and fortresses – could symbolize the things in which we place our trust. House could be safety, harbor could be livelihood or resources, and fortresses could be leadership or security.

God would remove these things to show the futility of trusting in the works of their hands.

We could learn from this today. God gives us all these things, but our primary focus, the source of our security, should be in Him alone.

In God's mercy, He tells them that their devastation has a definitive time frame – 70 years. After that time, they will return to their trade, interestingly enough compared to a prostitute. At first glance, it appears that Tyre would return to their old ways and learn nothing from the judgment.

Then we get to verse 18 where we see that Tyre's fortune would be given to the Lord and would benefit God's people. I can't say whether or not this is because the city of Tyre had learned from the judgment and worshipped the Lord or whether they were paying tribute to God's people; either is a possibility. I'd like to think it's the former, but struggle to reconcile the comparison to the prostitute – a common reference to idolatry – with a nation that had truly turned to follow God.

Whatever the motivation, it's clear that God's judgment of Tyre changes them. Even if they're being forced to give God their profits, they are not the same as they previously were.

When we go through hardships, we can choose to respond in a variety of ways. We can allow it to harden us, making us bitter or angry. We can wallow in self-pity. We can blame God. Or we can allow God to work in and through us, molding us into the image of Jesus.

Isaiah 24

1. From this chapter, what impresses, stands out, or convicts you?

2. Isaiah 24:1-3
   a. What do you learn about this time of devastation from these verses?

   b. Why do you think Isaiah ended verse 3 with "the Lord has spoken this word"?

3. Isaiah 24:4-13
   a. What are the reasons given for this devastation?

   b. How do you see the things listed in these verses happening in our world right now?

   c. What do you think is being said in verse 13?

d. Keeping in mind that we live under the new covenant in Christ's blood, how might you be guilty of breaking the everlasting covenant God made with you?

4. Isaiah 24:14-20
   a. Verses 14-16a are in stark contrast with the surrounding verses. Why might they have been inserted here and how do they fit with the messages on either side of them?

   b. What are some ways in which you can exalt the Lord, regardless of your circumstances?

   c. On the heels of the praise in 16a, Isaiah mourns. Why is he lamenting?

   d. Do you see the events in verses 17-20 occurring in our world today? If so, in what specific ways?

5. Isaiah 24:21-23
   a. To whom do you think verses 21-22 refer?

b. Why do you think the moon and sun are referenced in verse 23? What does this tell you about the Lord's reign?

c. What are some evidences that the Lord reigns in your life?

Chapter 24 – Thoughts and Considerations

It's hard to look at chapters like this, isn't it? We like focusing on God's blessings: grace and forgiveness, unconditional love, mercy, peace, and joy.

Too often we forget the fact that if God is good, He must also be just. There must be consequences for sin and punishment for unrepentance.

The whole earth suffers because of the sin of man (Gen 3:17, Isaiah 24:5-6, 19-20, Romans 8:18-22). In fact, Romans makes it clear the earth itself is looking forward to God's judgment and cleansing from sin. That judgment will be devastating, but necessary and perfectly just, for God will always be true to His righteous character.

If we're honest, most of us want justice for others and grace for ourselves. We want the murderers, child molesters, abusive, dishonest, and corrupt to "get what's coming to them" but want mercy for those "harmless" little sins that we and other "good" people commit.

The problem is that sin is sin.

God doesn't differentiate. There is no points system, no hierarchy that grades some sins as worse than others. Now from a human perspective, I think we'd all agree that murder is worse than a lie of omission, but to God all sin is equally wicked and deserving of judgment.

Praise God for Jesus and the cross, who took the judgment for all of us who call on Him!

Verse 2 makes it clear that none are exempt from the coming wrath. It doesn't matter what the profession or social standing, people of all walks of life will experience the impact of God's just judgment. I'm not sure where Christians fall in this list, but we can hold confidently to the promise that we are saved from eternal judgment (Romans 8:1), even if we experience some of the effects of God's judgment on sin in the world. This life is a very small blip on the radar compared to what comes after.

Anytime I see a declaration like "the Lord has spoken!" at the end of verse 3, I take note. Personally, I see this as God placing an emphasis on what has just been said – in essence, saying that this message is from Him and it will happen.

If you're like me, dozens of things popped into mind as you looked at the charges against mankind in verse 5.

God's instructions are twisted on a daily basis, often by those who claim to be Christian. Anytime we take a verse out of context or try to make it fit what we want it to mean, we are twisting God's instructions. When we pick and choose what we want to believe out of Scripture, we are twisting God's instructions. Anytime we accept something our culture says is right but God's word says is wrong, we are not being "tolerant" or "accepting", we are condoning sin and are twisting God's instructions.

That's one reason why it's so important to spend time studying God's word – it's the best way to discern truth from error. I heard an analogy somewhere that experts in detecting counterfeit money recognize fake bills by studying the real thing. The same applies to the truth. Don't waste time studying what is not true to try to figure out the truth – focus on the truth found in Scripture and let that reveal falsehood to you.

This is also a strong warning against buying into the lie that truth is relative. It's not. Truth, by definition, is absolute. It cannot change. Don't believe me? Check out the definition of truth for yourself.

God's word is to be our ultimate authority for truth, for God Himself is truth (John 14:6) and does not lie (Hebrews 6:18). Further, since we are made in the image of God, He has imprinted right and wrong on our hearts. Scripture tells us that mankind instinctively knows right from wrong (Romans 1-2), although for many people, sin has so dulled the senses that they have difficulty discerning it.

The effects of all of this are shown in the following verses: destruction, famine, absence of joy, no cause for celebration, chaos, security issues, violence and rioting, and devastation. None of these were part of God's initial design for us, but are the results of our sin.

Yet, as always, God preserves a remnant (v 13).

There are several reasons why this remnant might be praising God in verses 14-16. They may be praising God's mercy upon them. It might be because He sustained them during times of persecution. It might be because they finally saw His justice on wickedness and on those who mistreated or oppressed them.

Regardless of the cause, one thing is clear. Those of us who have placed our faith in Jesus, who are viewed by God as righteous because of Christ's sacrifice on our behalf, always have cause to give God thanks and praise.

No matter our circumstances, we can praise God, for He is with us and has saved us for all eternity. That is truly good news!

To me, it appears that the latter half of verse 16 snaps back to the present. Isaiah had witnessed the future judgment and the praise of the redeemed, but for now, all he sees around him is the trouble. He may also be mourning the coming judgment, for many people will perish when they refuse to turn to God for their salvation. There will be no escaping God's wrath when it finally comes.

Verses 21-22 address specific groups and their punishments. The gods in the heavens may refer to false gods or those who set themselves up as gods, or it may refer to demonic beings (who were formerly angels, hence the heavens reference). The proud rulers are possibly those who are heavy and oppressive and – since judgment is coming upon them – are clearly ones who do not follow the Lord.

What follows the judgment is truly amazing.

The sun and moon will fade as God reigns. We will no longer have need of their light, for God Himself will provide all the light we'll ever need. This theme is repeated in other end times prophecies including Isaiah 60:19 and Revelation 22:5.

For those of us who believe in Jesus, this will be a great and glorious thing. For all who don't, it will be a dreadful and horrible thing. The time for warning others of the coming judgment is now. In order to fully appreciate the good news, we have to fully understand the bad news: that we're all sinners deserving of judgment and have no hope apart from Christ.

With whom can you share both the good and bad news today? You may not have tomorrow, so seize the moment!

Isaiah 25

1. From this chapter, what impresses, stands out, or convicts you?

2. Isaiah 25:1-5
   a. How would the knowledge that God had planned things long ago be a comfort to Isaiah?

   b. Why do you think Isaiah is rejoicing over the destruction listed in verse 2?

   c. Why would this destruction make strong people honor God and ruthless nations revere Him?

   d. Explain what you think is meant by the imagery in verses 4b-5.

   e. How has God proven Himself to be a refuge and shelter in your own life?

3. Isaiah 25:6-9

   a. In what ways could these verses be pointing toward Christ?

   b. What might be meant by the shroud and sheet (in NIV) in verse 7?

   c. To whom might God be calling you to declare His salvation and trustworthiness?

4. Isaiah 25:10-12

   a. Do you think these verses were written specifically to Moab or was Moab used allegorically? Why?

   b. What warnings do you discern in these verses? Which is most personally relevant to you today?

   c. What do you think is meant by the reference to the swimmer in verse 11?

d. Why do you think these verses were placed here (immediately following this passage of praise)?

e. In what high fortified walls (v 12, NIV) or cleverness of your own hands (v 11, NIV) are you trusting?

Chapter 25 – Thoughts and Considerations

This chapter is a welcome refreshment from the chapters of judgment we've been looking at, isn't it?

This chapter shows the perfect control of God. Isaiah saw God's plan and the eventual outcome, and praised God for it.

We, too, can rest in the knowledge that God has ultimate control, even though the world seems to be spinning out of control all around us. We may not see His control, nor understand His purposes in allowing the seeming chaos, but we can trust the truths we find in His word and know that He truly does have full control.

The contrast between verses 3 and 4 is startling. The strong peoples and ruthless nations would respect God for His mighty power and sovereign control; yet with the poor and needy, God would prove Himself to be a shelter and refuge. Just as a storm has no impact on a solidly built wall (v 4) and heat dissipates when shaded (v 5), no one can come against those under God's protection and succeed. Yes, bad things happen to God's children all the time, but ultimately those who belong to God have the victory, even if they have to wait until the next life to claim it.

The beauty of verses 6-8 is found in their inclusiveness. The word "all" is used 5 times in those 2 verses (in the classic NIV, anyway). The promises contained here are truly for all people, not just Israel.

My first thought when reading verse 6 is the wedding feast of the Lamb (Revelation 19:7-9). I'm not sure if that is specifically what is being referenced, but the similarities are strong.

Verses 7-8 could point to the cross. Jesus was sacrificed on a hill, not a mountain, but with His death He destroyed the power of sin (perhaps symbolized by the shroud of death in these verses) and swallowed up death forever. Our shame and disgrace have been forever removed (v 8) because Jesus took the penalty for our sin upon Himself.

The shroud may also symbolize a shroud of the mind that darkens our thinking and keeps us from enjoying a relationship with God (2 Corinthians 3:14-16, Ephesians 4:18).

God ends this promise with the words "The Lord has spoken" – which, as previously discussed feels like an official seal of God placed upon these words. We can count on them to happen, just as God said, in God's perfect timing.

The chapter ends with a warning for Moab. This could literally mean Moab or Moab could be a symbol for all who don't choose God. Since they're specifically listed here, I believe that Moab is the primary recipient of this warning, while also being used symbolically. Moab's pride is mentioned in several other passages – Isaiah 16:6, Jeremiah 48:29-30, and Zephaniah 2:8-10 – so they might've been notorious for their pride.

The reference to a swimmer puzzles me a little bit, although a swimmer trusts in his strength to move through the water and keep from drowning, which would tie in to the end of this verse that references Moab's failing, despite the "cleverness of their hands."

It might also tie back to the end of the previous verse and the idea of them being trampled in manure. Perhaps they're trying to swim in the "manure" – which creates a disgusting mental image, I know – but would very successfully illustrate the futility of their efforts.

This is a strong warning to us.

In this chapter, Isaiah highlights God's attributes, His sovereignty and control, shows how God cares for His own, then ends with a warning against trusting in the works of our hands and the trappings of physical safety (high walls, v 12). We can choose to place our trust in our jobs, families, financial security, the government, leaders, good health, even the spiritual gifts God gives us, but if we don't acknowledge that all these things come from God and that He alone is our stability and security in an unstable world, then we might find ourselves learning the lesson of Moab.

Isaiah 26

1. From this chapter, what impresses, stands out, or convicts you?

2. Isaiah 26:1-6
   a. In what ways is God's salvation like a strong city?

   b. What are the prerequisites to being kept in God's perfect peace?

   c. In what situation do you need to fix your eyes upon the Lord, the Rock Eternal?

   d. What truths do you learn from the destruction of the lofty by the poor in verses 5-6?

3. Isaiah 26:7-11
   a. What do you think verse 7 is promising to those who pursue righteousness?

b. What might waiting for the Lord look like?

c. Is God truly the desire of your heart? In what areas do your desires need to change?

d. Summarize the message in verses 10-11. With whom do you feel called to share God's grace?

4. Isaiah 26:12-19
   a. To whom might "other lords" refer? How did these "lords" compare to God?

   b. What are some ways in which God might have enlarged the nation?

   c. What principles do you see in verses 16-19?

   d. What empty striving exists in your life? Where are you placing hope in something that lacks the power to deliver?

5. Isaiah 26:20-21

    a.Do you think these verses are saying we can hide from God's justice? If not, what do you think they are saying?

    b.Could there be a situation in your life right now where God is calling you to hide rather than fight?

Chapter 26 – Thoughts and Considerations

The comparison of God to a strong city gives us such a good image to which to cling, especially when times are tough. In those days, a strong city was surrounded by thick stone walls to prevent enemies from breaking through. Those walls were intended to stand, even during times of war, to protect all who sought shelter within.

Unlike those walls, which sometimes did fall during battle, God provides perfect security and eternal protection against the fires of hell. No one can breach or undo God's salvation – it is eternally secure in Christ. We only have one small part to play in this process and it's found in verses 3-4: Trust in God.

Verses 5-6 show God's dealings with the proud and the humble. In this life, the proud rule, often at the expense of the poor, but in times to come God will humble the proud and elevate the poor and oppressed, for whom God consistently throughout Scripture shows special affection.

Verse 7 is one that we have to be careful not to take out of context. It would be so easy to use that verse to proclaim an "easy street" gospel, that if you choose Jesus, life will come up perfect every time. Scripture proves that such a thing is not true. In fact, Jesus promises us we will experience trouble (John 16:33).

So what is this verse saying?

I think it's pointing to the surety of walking in God's paths. If we do what is right, it's like walking on level ground. Think about how hard it is to walk a trail that is full of boulders and roots, trees, and shrubs. You're likely to roll your ankle, scrape your legs, maybe even be surprised by a wild animal emerging from the brush. Contrast that with a paved path – even one that might climb uphill at a steep incline. It's not that the trail is necessarily easy, but you can move with less fear for the ground beneath your feet is firm.

It's the same with walking in God's righteousness. It doesn't mean the path will be easy, but it will be firm for it is upheld by God Himself.

Verse 8 is a beautiful verse that describes how Christians are to live before the Lord. The NLT says: "Lord, we show our trust in You by obeying Your laws; our heart's desire is to glorify Your Name."

What an amazing thing it would be if we all lived that! I think it's good for us to take a moment to really dwell on this. What does my level of obedience say about my trust in God? Do others see it? Or do they see me doing my own thing for my own glory? Is glorifying God really my heart's desire? Is it yours?

I also like what the NIV says in this verse. It's similar, but with a key difference: the idea of waiting. "Yes, Lord, walking in the way of Your laws, we wait for You; Your Name and renown are the desire of our hearts."

At first glance, it almost appears that these verses are saying different things, doesn't it? After all, walking in God's ways is active, but waiting seems passive. But when we stop and really consider it, not only are the translations saying the same thing, they're also complementing each other.

Biblical waiting is not a passive, sit-on-your-hands-and-do-nothing kind of waiting. It involves action. Biblical waiting involves a continual walk with God, seeking Him, following His leading (usually one step at a time), and continuing to do the last work that He called us to until He calls us to stop.

While we "wait", we actually carry on.

Perhaps one of the clearest examples of Biblical waiting occurs in Acts 1-2. Jesus told His disciples to wait in Jerusalem for the promised Holy Spirit. The disciples obey, but they weren't idle. They appointed another man to replace Judas as one of the twelve. They spent time in prayer, seeking the Lord's will.

Another good example is when Paul intended to go into Asia to preach the gospel, but the Holy Spirit stopped him from going there (Acts 16:6-10). Did he and Silas just kick back and relax until God showed them the next step? No! They continued travelling in the area where they had been ministering until God gave them a vision to direct their next steps.

A few other places where Scripture combines action with waiting include Psalm 119:165-168 and Hosea 12:6.

The verses that follow highlight the differences in response from the godly and the wicked. The godly learn and seek to please God, but the wicked do not learn, no matter how often they are told or how many lessons God sends their way.

It culminates in the example of a woman giving birth. No matter how much people might strive, we are unable to gain eternal life on our own. Our efforts are as empty as a pregnant woman who gives birth to wind rather than a living baby. Salvation is a work that only God can do.

The chapter ends with a warning to all of God's people to hide while His judgment falls.

We typically think of hiding as a cowardly or selfish action, yet that is not always the case. There are times when hiding or retreating is the most prudent course of action. Sometimes it can be a time of healing or lead us to self-examination and repentance.

Some notable examples of retreat or hiding in Scripture include:

- Noah, who hid in the ark from the flood (Genesis 6-8)
- Joseph, who fled from Potiphar's wife and the temptation she presented (Genesis 39)
- Elijah, who hid in the desert from King Ahab and Jezebel (1 Kings 17:1-6)
- The early church, who hid from persecutors and fled danger (multiple places in Acts)

If you're familiar with your Bible history, you know how God used these times to work out His will in the lives of the individual(s) and the nation. For example, had the early church not suffered the intense persecution, they may not have dispersed, which spread the gospel across the known world at an unprecedented pace.

There is no hiding from God or escaping His justice, but there are times where He calls His people to separate themselves from the evil surrounding them.

So if you sense God telling you to pull back in a certain area, particularly if it's one that presents spiritual danger or temptation, don't hesitate to obey. He might be saving you from yourself or sparing you judgment that is coming in a particular area.

Isaiah 27

1. From this chapter, what impresses, stands out, or convicts you?

2. Isaiah 27:1-6
   a. Who or what do you think is being referred to as Leviathan in verse 1?

   b. In what ways could this verse also symbolize the power of God over adversity or sin in your own life?

   c. Who is the vineyard of the Lord? To whom or what might the thorns refer?

   d. How do verses 4-5 demonstrate both God's justice and His mercy?

   e. What might be meant by the promise given in verse 6?

f. In what ways have we seen fulfillment of this promise today?

g. In what areas of your life are you producing good fruit? What briers and thorns might be hindering your witness?

3. Isaiah 27:7-9
   a. How do verses 7-8 prove God's compassion and grace for His fallen people?

   b. What responsibility did the people have in response to God's removal of their sins?

   c. What idols do you need to crush in your life today?

4. Isaiah 27:10-13
   a. To whom do you think verses 10-11 refer?

   b. In what ways did the people lack understanding? How do you fall into the same trap?

c. What is especially meaningful to you from the promises given in verses 12-13?

d. How might you offer genuine worship to God throughout your day?

Chapter 27 – Thoughts and Considerations

The reference to Leviathan is an interesting one, isn't it? Leviathan was a sea monster (possibly mythical) that may be used symbolically here for Satan, the enemies of God's people, or evil.

It's interesting to note the verbs used to refer to Leviathan's actions – gliding and coiling. To me, gliding brings to mind smooth and stealthy, like a snake slithering through long grass. You may not see it coming until it's too late. Coiling carries the idea of being poised for attack. Combining these, I see Leviathan as being sneaky and dangerous... but still no match for God. God will act against it and triumph, sparking a song of praise.

This is the second of Isaiah's vineyard songs. There's a vast difference between the two, specifically in a few key areas.

- Protection: The vineyard in chapter 5 had its hedge removed, walls broken, and the vines were trampled and destroyed (5:5), yet this one is guarded by God Himself and zealously protected from harm (27:3-4)
- Nourishment: The chapter 5 vineyard was parched, for the clouds were commanded not to rain (5:6), yet this one is watered continually (27:3)
- Briers and thorns: The chapter 5 vineyard was a wasteland filled with briers and thorns (5:6), yet in this vineyard, God will burn away any that grow (27:4)

Verse 5 is interesting... God gives "them" a choice. When I read it, it almost appears that it's the briers and thorns that are being given a choice here, which brings up some interesting possibilities.

Perhaps the briers and thorns reflect the enemies of God's people and God is offering them a chance to join His people rather than oppose them. It could also refer to those among God's people who are willfully walking in sin. God is giving them the option to come to Him for refuge, to make peace with Him, before He burns the sin from their lives through fire.

However you read it, the offer of mercy is unmistakable. God is always lovingly calling people to come to Him.

His people will be restored and, even though He disciplined them, they still had it easier than the other nations. God compares what happened to them to what happened to others and highlights the cleansing power of His judgment.

The people's guilt is "atoned for" (v 9) and the result would be the destruction of the idolatrous altars and pagan symbols throughout the land.

I'm not completely sure to whom verses 10-11 refer. I'm thinking (perhaps erroneously) that it refers to Jerusalem, maybe all of Judah, during the time of exile. The city (cities) would have been desolate, animals would have overrun the land, and the people remaining would have been weak and helpless (symbolized by the woman making a fire with broken twigs and the people lacking understanding).

But this time is only for a short while – God would bring them back. I love that He gathers them one by one and they return, worshipping Him in Jerusalem once again.

God has done the same for us. He calls each of us by name, drawing us one by one. Will you be one who is described as lacking understanding? Or will you respond as the people do in verse 13, approaching God in true worship?

Isaiah 28

1. From this chapter, what impresses, stands out, or convicts you?

2. Isaiah 28:1-8
   a. What remarkable differences do you see between the people referenced in verses 5-6 and the people referenced in the rest of these verses?

   b. What might be the reason for the repeated mention of alcohol in this passage?

   c. What fading beauty has drawn your attention away from God – who alone is to be our pride?

3. Isaiah 28:9-13
   a. What do these verses reveal about Isaiah's audience?

   b. What warnings do you see in these verses?

4. Isaiah 28:14-22

   a. What do you think is meant by the people's boast in
      verse 15? What does it reveal about them?

   b. Why might God have included the message of verses 16-
      17 where He did?

   c. In what false securities might you be placing your trust?
      How solid is the foundation of your life?

   d. To what "strange work" and "alien task" do you think
      Isaiah is referring in verse 21?

5. Isaiah 28:23-29

   a. What do you learn from this farming illustration? How
      does it tie in to the rest of this chapter?

   b. What changes might occur in our nation if we followed
      God's instructions and lived according to His standards?

   c. What does your life reveal about how much value you
      place upon God's perfect ways?

Chapter 28 – Thoughts and Considerations

This chapter shows the divide between the remnant (those who follow God) and the rest (who are under God's judgment). Most of the chapter focuses on the latter group, serving as a warning to them to turn back now.

These first few verses have a heavy focus on alcohol and drunkenness. Possibly this is intended to be taken literally – after all, the Bible does speak against drunkenness (Luke 21:33-35, Romans 13:13, Ephesians 5:18) – but I suspect a larger message is contained here and the alcohol references are symbolic of all worldly overindulgences.

Wine was a necessity in those days because of the lack of readily available clean water. It appears that people didn't always moderate their consumption, however.

Let's consider this for a moment: when someone has too much to drink, they say and do things they normally wouldn't say or do. Their inhibitions are lowered. They act without thought or care for the consequences. Often, they don't really care about the things that truly matter.

Do you see the correlation?

When we pursue worldly things over heavenly ones, our focus is not on what is lasting. We're more likely to act in self-interest, with little to no thought of how our words or actions might impact others. We seek to satisfy the temporal over the eternal.

What's shocking here is the various people who are included in this group of drunkards: priests and prophets, who should have been leading by example. Their drunkenness, taken either literally or symbolically (or both) caused them to stagger when seeing visions (I take that to mean that their visions were not accurate) and stumble when rendering justice (make unjust decisions).

Verse 8 clearly shows that the evidence of the sin would be everywhere – nothing was left untouched.

What a sobering thought when we consider our own sin!

Sin impacts more than just the person committing it; it ripples out from us, touching those around us. Some sins have more ripples than others, but never doubt that every sin has a ripple effect to some degree.

The contrast between the two groups of people in these verses is stark. The first group, the drunkards, are a fading flower (v 4) and a trampled wreath (v 3) while the remnant find their value in the Lord, who will be to them a glorious crown and a beautiful wreath (v 5). For the remnant, God gives them what they need to do what He has called them to do, whether it's to render judgments or to stand guard or fight (v 6).

Verses 9-13 are a little mysterious. We see in their attitude that they didn't understand... and possibly had no desire to understand. These verses might even be used sarcastically – perhaps the people had said these things to make fun of the prophets' warnings. It could also possibly display the attitude of the priests and leaders, who might have been offended by the simplicity of the prophets' messages. It might also refer to the fact that the people lacked understanding (perhaps because they didn't want to understand), so God would speak to them in simple terms, over and over, as if teaching a child.

You might have come up with other alternatives, too. Whatever the meaning, since the people refused to hear the message from God Himself, He would use foreigners, like the Assyrians and the Babylonians, to deliver His message through force (v 11).

The covenant with death (mentioned in verses 15 and 18) might refer to the alliances the people tried to make with other nations, nations who had at one time been – or would become – their enemies. Judah made an alliance with Egypt (Isaiah 20:5-6, 30:1-3) and Assyria (2 Kings 16:7-9), both nations that caused substantial human casualties.

It's not bad to ask for help when we need it or to work in

cooperation with others to achieve a common goal, but the people sinned in these instances for several reasons: God had expressly told them NOT to form these alliances and the people formed them because they didn't trust God to protect them.

In the middle of this section, God tucks in these beautiful verses about whom we should trust: the precious cornerstone, whom we know from the New Testament to be Jesus Christ (Acts 4:11). Anyone who puts their trust in someone other than Him will have no refuge or hiding place and will be overtaken by the coming judgment.

The strange work and alien task (v 21) might refer to God working *against* His people. In the past, He'd protected and acted on behalf of His people, but His people had broken the covenant and turned against Him.

Yet His mercy is evident. In verse 22, the people are warned again to change or things would only grow worse.

The chapter ends with this farming illustration. With the heavily agricultural economy, the people would have understood the meaning of this better than many of us do today.

There are many applications for us. The farmer knows what steps to take to get a crop, but where does this knowledge come from? It comes from experience and watching how God works in nature. All knowledge ultimately comes from the Lord.

The farmer also does all he can, but at some point his job is done. All he can do is trust that God will bring the rain and grow the plants. We can do all the right things, but God is the one who brings work to fruition. Without Him, there is no harvest – literal or spiritual.

Plowing and threshing have a purpose... as does judgment. Both last only for a time.

Different crops require different tactics and processes. The same is true with people. God treats each of us as individuals, giving us just what we need to achieve the desired end product.

This is truly good news for us! It means my walk with the Lord, my work for Him, doesn't need to look like yours and your walk and work shouldn't look like mine. Just as God made us different, so He deals with each of us differently. God sees us as the unique creation He made us to be, not carbon copies of each other. What a wonderful, personal God we have!

Isaiah 29

1. From this chapter, what impresses, stands out, or convicts you?

2. Isaiah 29:1-8
   a. What would be the results of God's judgment on Ariel/Jerusalem?

   b. How would God's treatment of His people differ from the wrath shown her enemies?

   c. Can you think of a time when God sheltered or saved you from those who wished you harm?

3. Isaiah 29:9-16
   a. Why would God tell the people to be sightless and drunk (v 9)? Why would He seal their eyes and cover their heads (v 10)?

b. What examples come to mind of how our society is suffering from this same thing today?

c. What warnings do you receive in these verses? Which is most applicable to you right now?

d. How do people try to hide their plans or actions from God? Where might you be guilty of doing this same thing?

4. Isaiah 29:17-24
   a. To what do you think the promises in verses 17-19 refer? How are these same promises applicable to Christians today?

   b. What are some modern examples of the evils listed in verses 20-21?

   c. How have the prophecies in this section already been fulfilled in part? When do you think this prophecy will see complete fulfillment?

d. Why do you think seeing their children (v 23) would cause the people to acknowledge and revere God?

e. In what practical ways can you keep God's name holy, acknowledge Him, and stand in awe of Him as you go about your daily life?

Chapter 29 – Thoughts and Considerations

This chapter is a beautiful illustration of God's character – it shows His divine justice and righteous judgment on sin, His continuous call to the sinner to repent, and His mercy on those who choose Him.

Ariel is similar to the Hebrew word for altar hearth; fitting, since Jerusalem was the site of the temple and God's altar. Perhaps it is used here somewhat ironically, since the people had long since turned from worshipping God alone. Perhaps He used it specifically to remind them of how they should be revering Him instead of spurning Him.

We see that His judgment would humble them completely, so that their voices would come from low in the dust (v 4).

What's interesting about this, though, is that the same fate awaited their enemies. Verse 5 says that they (the enemies) would be crushed like the finest of dust. Yet unlike verse 4, it doesn't mention voices, perhaps indicating that their enemies would be unable to speak, for God would totally wipe them out.

Sadly enough, it appears that the people choose blindness and stupidity to the wisdom and blessings God offers them (v 9).

Verse 10 sure is sobering; God left them to their choices. It's a similar thing to what He did in hardening Pharaoh's heart in the time of the exodus. For the first 5 plagues, Pharaoh hardened his own heart (Exodus 7:22, 8:15, 8:19, 8:32, and 9:7); only after his heart was sufficiently self-hardened does Scripture say that God hardened his heart (Exodus 9:12).

Such is the danger of allowing any hardness of heart to enter in. God continually calls us to Himself, but a time will come when He will leave us to our own choices and the consequences they carry.

We must be careful to be sensitive to His leading so that we don't become like Pharaoh or the Israelite people in this passage who refused to even try to hear the Lord.

Verses 11-12 might refer to their flimsy excuses for not listening to the message God gave them: the scroll is sealed, maybe indicating that they were too lazy to try to understand or too comfortable in their sin to want to understand. The excuse of not being able to read is also used, which could correlate to the message being too difficult to understand, accept, and/or obey.

Jesus applied the following verses to the Pharisees in Mark 7:6-8. They refused to listen to His teachings – the very words of God – clinging instead to their man-made rules, traditions, and ideas of what following God should look like.

I think the modern church is in danger of this very thing. Remember that the "church" is actually the people who attend it, not the building or organization, so this is directed at us as believers, not any particular denomination.

It's easy to get into our religious habits and patterns; we sing the right songs, take communion, bow our heads, attend out of obligation, maybe even drop a little money in the offering, but still have our hearts far from God. I see this passage as a challenge to examine my heart. Why do I do the things I do? Is it to earn extra points with God (as if that were possible)? Or is it out of genuine love and worship for the Almighty One who knows me and loves me anyway?

Jesus certainly fulfilled verse 14. I'm sure that verse has had multiple fulfillments throughout time, but since we were just looking at Jesus in the preceding section, I was struck by how much this verse described His ministry. He did amazing things that truly did astound the Pharisees. On many occasions He silenced them with the wisdom and depth of His teachings, making their own wisdom appear to be foolishness by comparison. Even the "uneducated" population noticed the depth and authority of His teachings (Matt 7:29, 9:8, Mark 1:27, Luke 4:32-36)!

Verses 15-16 are almost laughable as they discuss people who try to hide their deeds from omniscient God. God sees all, so He not only knows what we do, He knows what we're thinking about doing! To think we can somehow sneak something past Him is ludicrous.

Yet people do that on a regular basis, don't they? How often do we hold back certain parts of our lives from God?

Perhaps it's your viewing choices. Maybe it's the music you listen to. It could be the things you choose to read, the games you play, the way you spend your free time, or your favorite leisure activities. Not that any of these things are bad in themselves, but there are bad options out there, things you wouldn't choose if Jesus Himself were sitting physically in your living room and you knew He would see/hear them, too. For the sake of this argument, we'll ignore the reality that since the Holy Spirit lives inside us, He does see them.

It might be as simple as making our own plans without praying about it or giving God any consideration in our decisions. Doing so is essentially the same as being the clay pot that denies its Creator.

Verses 18-19 again see a fulfillment at the coming of Christ, but I think we'll see a deeper fulfillment when He returns one day. Certainly the events listed in verses 20-24 have not been realized in full yet, but what an amazing thing that will one day be!

Seeing their children (v 23) would point the people toward God because children symbolize the future. In seeing the children, the people would see that they actually have a future and that God has been faithful to keep every promise He made. God's faithfulness, His power, and His care will cause people to turn from their sin (the wayward, v 24) and stop complaining so they can truly listen to the words of Almighty God.

Isaiah 30-31

1. From these chapters, what impresses, stands out, or convicts you?

2. Isaiah 30:1-7
   a. Why do you think Israel turned to Egypt for help? Why was this choice somewhat ironic considering past experiences between these two nations?

   b. Why was God upset with His people for seeking help from Egypt?

   c. What or whom might be an Egypt in your own life? In what situation have you sought outside help from this source rather than seeking the Lord?

3. Isaiah 30:8-17
   a. What are some reasons that the people might have responded as they did in verses 10-11?

b. How do you see these same attitudes in our culture today? In our churches? In your own life?

c. How did God deal lovingly with His people, even in the face of their blatant rebellion?

4. Isaiah 30:18-33
   a. In what ways might the "bread of adversity" and the "water of affliction" have been a blessing in disguise?

   b. Why would the people finally cast aside the idols to which they had clung for so long?

   c. What do you learn about the Lord from the descriptions given in this passage?

   d. Why do you think Isaiah made repeated references to the Lord's mouth (lips, tongue, breath, voice)?

5. Isaiah 31:1-9
   a. What attributes of God stand out in this chapter?

b. Why do you think Isaiah reminded the people that God "does not take back His words" (v 2)?

c. What significance do you see in the last two lines of this chapter — that the Lord's "fire is in Zion" and His "furnace is in Jerusalem"?

d. In what battles or trials have you clearly witnessed God taking action on your behalf?

Chapter 30-31 – Thoughts and Considerations

It was a lot of reading, but these two chapters really tie together well, don't they?

These chapters likely deal with an instance – recorded only in passing (2 Kings 18:21, Isaiah 30:2 and 6-7, Isaiah 36:6, Ezekiel 29:6-7) – in which King Hezekiah sought help from Egypt to stand against the Assyrians. From this chapter, as well as the references above, we can gather that Hezekiah sent great riches to Egypt to buy their support, but Egypt failed to be any help in times of trouble.

It's interesting to me that the sin here was not in seeking Egypt's help, but in not consulting God first. Now had the people consulted God, He would have told them they weren't to seek Egypt's help (30:1), but the main sin here was that the people forged ahead with their own plans rather than seeking God's plan for them.

I don't know about you, but I cringe a little when I read that because I know how often I do the exact same thing.

Be honest with yourself. How often do you examine a situation, make your plans, and proceed without giving God a second thought, much less asking Him what He would have you do?

I'm not talking about the little in-the-minute decisions like "what should I have for lunch?" but the bigger decisions like "what should I do with my day?" or "how should I spend my money?" or "should I find a new job / go back to school / get married / have a child?" type of questions. The bigger the decision, the more we need God's guidance to make it.

Too often, though, I think we make our plans and ask God to bless them. That's backwards from the Biblical model of planning!

The next verses give us the people's response to the messages they were given.

The people were so hardened that they didn't even want to hear God's words. They wanted to hear only feel-good messages, not the truth about their sin or the coming judgment.

In fact, they go so far as to say "... stop confronting us with the Holy One of Israel!"

Does that sound familiar? Think about the popularity of health and wealth gospels in our culture today. Think about what happens in a church when a pastor delivers a socially unpopular message – perhaps taking a firm stand on a hot button issue that is clearly spelled out in the Bible but is not politically correct today – and people get offended or leave the church because they don't like hearing the truth.

Our culture is okay with us believing in God, but when we declare truths from the Bible that the culture doesn't like – that Jesus is the only way of salvation, for example (John 14:6, Romans 10:9-10, 1 Thessalonians 5:9) – we are suddenly labeled as judgmental, narrow-minded, and unloving.

As the children of God, we should follow Jesus' example in all things, speaking the truth in love, with the desire to see people turn to God. If we don't, we'll never impact the culture around us.

God tells them plainly that the lies they were wanting to hear and the falsehood they were believing would collapse around them (vs 12-14).

I love how God tells them what they really need and what He longs to give them, then contrasts it with what they think they want. Did you notice that He gives them exactly what they say they want? In verse 16, they want to flee, so God says that they will indeed flee. Yet it won't be in the manner they want. They will flee in terror, pursued by enemies who are stronger and swifter than they are.

They chose the path they would end up walking. God desired a different path for them, but loved them enough to give them the choice – much like He does with each of us today.

In spite of their choices, God would act on their behalf and restore them (vs 18-21). He would give them good leaders and teachers who would guide them in the right way. I wonder if the "voice behind you" in verse 21 is a reference to the Holy Spirit, who guides believers in the way of the Lord if we'll only stop and listen.

The result would be that the people would finally rid themselves of their idols, likely seeing the contrast between the helpless idols and all-powerful God. God would send abundant water and the land would be plentiful.

The reference to light (the moon and sun) in verse 26 might be indicative of the spiritual state of the nation – following God's cleansing, God's light would shine, banishing the spiritual darkness that had cloaked the land for so long. It would be in the midst of this incredible light that God would bring healing on His wounded people.

There are repeated references to the Lord's mouth – whether it's His lips and tongue (v 27), His breath (v 28, 33), or His voice (v 30-31). A few thoughts on the symbolism behind this are that God is so powerful that He can bring victory without lifting a hand (although He does bring His arm down in verse 30, perhaps symbolic of passing judgment – like pounding a gavel in a courtroom).

It could also be to highlight the importance of listening to the Lord. If His breath, His lips, His tongue, and His words can bring down a nation as powerful as Assyria, shouldn't we take heed of everything He says?

30:33 mentions Topheth, which was evidently a place where people sacrificed to pagan gods (2 Kings 23:10, Jeremiah 7:31-32). Scripture often mentions the sacrifice of children, something we know God abhors (Jeremiah 7:31).

Chapter 31 really reiterates the main points of chapter 30. God alone is to be our first defender and the things He says will all come to pass (possibly the meaning of "He does not take back His words" in verse 2).

The Egyptians would fall, being of no help to Judah, but God would not be frightened by the Assyrian army. He would defend His people.

Verses 8-9 could refer to when God destroyed the Assyrian army (Isaiah 37:36 and 2 Kings 19:35) or it could refer to the broader fall of the entire empire at a later date, although God used the Medo-Persians to accomplish that task so the reference to them not falling by a human sword doesn't exactly fit.

I love how this chapter ends. In spite of the people's continuous rebellion and sin, God still chooses to identify with them and make His dwelling in Jerusalem (fire in Zion, furnace in Jerusalem).

This is good news for us.

Regardless of what we've done, if we have trusted Jesus for salvation the Holy Spirit lives within us. Just as God did not leave Jerusalem, He will not leave us (John 14:15-18). His promises are eternal.

Isaiah 32

1. From this chapter, what impresses, stands out, or convicts you?

2. Isaiah 32:1-8
   a. What would be the results of the good leadership God would establish?

   b. In what ways can you be like a shelter, refuge, and streams of water to the people around you?

   c. Do you think these verses point only to Christ? Why or why not?

   d. What are some ways we see fools and scoundrels (vs 6-7) at work today?

3. Isaiah 32:9-13
   a. In what were the complacent women placing their trust?

b. What are the dangers associated with such complacency?

c. What warnings do you find in this section for us today?

d. Where might God be calling you to shake off the bonds of complacency in your life?

4. Isaiah 32:14-20
   a. What difference would the outpouring of God's Spirit make upon the people and the land?

   b. Do you believe the outpouring of God's Spirit is in reference to a specific event or a general promise of blessings? Why?

   c. What problems, worries, or concerns do you need to surrender to God today to enjoy the peace and security His Spirit provides?

Chapter 32 – Thoughts and Considerations

This chapter has so many wonderful promises in it. It starts by promising a righteous king. This promise won't see total fulfillment until Christ rules, although there was partial fulfillment at His first coming. Depending upon when this chapter was written, it may have also seen some fulfillment in good human kings such as Hezekiah.

I take the mention of rulers to be people of a lower hierarchy who serve under the king, with the promise in verse 2 being in specific reference to them.

There's a deep spiritual application here, I believe.

Good rulers are essential and when those rulers submit to the King of Kings, they can be powerful sources of refreshing, stability, and shelter to those around them. These leaders don't have to just be pastors or missionaries, although they are certainly in this category, but can also be you and me.

We all lead someone, whether it's our families or children, friends, new believers, co-workers, or people in our churches. How do they see you? Do you pour God's love out on them, speak truth, encourage, and provide blessing? Or are you like bitter water that no one would want to drink?

For contrast, check out the description of fools and scoundrels in verses 6-7. May that never be true of any of us!

Sandwiched in the middle of this chapter is a strong warning against complacency. It's addressed specifically to women, yet is applicable to everyone.

The women in this passage appear to not care what's going on around them as long as they were able to maintain the lifestyle they enjoyed. God calls them to wake up and look around, to take action now before everything is stripped away.

Perhaps their complacency was out of a lack of awareness or perhaps they didn't really think that trouble would touch them. Maybe they'd even heard what God had to say and didn't believe it would come to pass. It appears they were relying upon the material – crops, abundance, wealth, appearance, and financial stability – rather than placing their trust in God.

This call against complacency is for us, too.

Similar complacency is very real and active today. We see it in the lack of concern for the poor, when people won't step in to help the abused or the victimized members of society, when we shrug off injustice in our legal system, and when we side with the rich or powerful even when they're wrong. Those are just a few ways that complacency has taken hold of our society. There are countless others.

Of even greater danger, though, is complacency in our faith.

Too often, we grow complacent in our walk with the Lord, which stagnates our growth. We're still saved, but we're too comfortable in our daily lives. We live as part of the world, rather than being separate from it when Jesus has clearly called us to live apart from the world (John 15:18-19, Romans 12:2).

Keep in mind that Satan wants us to be complacent in our faith, for when we are complacent, we are also ineffective for the kingdom. Be aware of what's going on and bold with the truth about Jesus, no matter how unpopular it is in societal circles.

The pouring out of the Spirit (v 15) brings abundance. It's possible that these verses are referring to the physical realm in which the people lived, for God often blesses us with physical gifts, but it no doubt also refers to the spiritual blessings that are ours when we live according to the Spirit.

God's Spirit makes our desert-like hearts fertile, full of the best things and richest blessings. Just as a fertile field produces a good harvest, so a Spirit-filled heart produces good spiritual fruit (Matthew 7:17-19, 12:33, Luke 6:43, Galatians 5:22, Colossians 1:10, James 3:17). Verses 16-18 mention some of these fruits: justice, righteousness, peace, quietness, confidence, safety, and rest.

We can see in verse 19 that this doesn't mean life around them is perfect, but that they find their security and comfort in the Lord, no matter what happens around them.

Can the same be said of you? How do you respond when the world around you unravels? Scripture promises that if we fix our eyes on God, trust Him, and live in His Spirit, we can enjoy the promises listed above, no matter our circumstances.

Isaiah 33

1. From this chapter, what impresses, stands out, or convicts you?

2. Isaiah 33:1-6
   a. To whom do you think verse 1 is directed? How would you tie it to the verses that follow?

   b. According to these verses, what are some of the benefits of trusting God?

   c. What is required to enjoy the security offered by God? In what practical ways could you put this into practice in your life today?

3. Isaiah 33:7-16
   a. Why might the message of verses 7-9 have been placed here?

b. What do verses 10-12 say to you?

c. What would be some of the responses when the Lord acted?

d. What specific examples come to mind of how our society accepts the things the righteous are told to reject in verse 15?

e. Where in your life might you be guilty of perpetrating – or at least tolerating – these same sins?

4. Isaiah 33:17-24
   a. What changes would occur when the people focused on the King in verse 17?

   b. What blessings would the people receive when they made God their judge, lawgiver, and king?

   c. To whom do you think verse 23 refers?

d. What significance do you find in the way Isaiah closes this chapter?

e. In what present situation do you need to simply fix your eyes upon the Lord?

Chapter 33 – Thoughts and Considerations

I feel like I say this a lot, but this chapter highlights the differences between God's treatment of His people and their enemies.

Depending upon the timeframe in which this was written, verse 1 may refer to Assyria or it might refer to Babylon.

Assyria seems like a viable option to me for a few reasons. First, each of these descriptions applies to them. Assyria wrought massive destruction on any nation they conquered. They made a treaty with King Hezekiah in 2 Kings 18:13-16, but verse 17 shows them trying to overtake Jerusalem anyway. It's possible that time elapses between verses 16 and 17, but it's also possible that Assyria took the tribute Hezekiah offered with no intention of stopping their attack.

The verses that follow highlight the character of God and the way He comes to the aid of His people.

These blessings are ours to claim as well!

God helps us in times of distress, has given us strength, a rich store of salvation and wisdom and knowledge, provides a sure foundation, and governs with justice and righteousness. The only things we have to do to experience these blessings are found in verses 2 and 6: wait (or long) for God and have the fear of the Lord.

Verses 7-9 may refer to the events described in 2 Kings 18:17-37 (also in Isaiah 36) when Assyrian officials, under Sennacherib's command, meet with Hezekiah's officials in an attempt to bully them into surrendering. We'll actually study this event in more detail when we get to chapter 36 so I won't go into it now, but Hezekiah's "great" plan for a peace treaty has failed because Assyria and Sennacherib would not uphold their end. Things looked very bleak in Jerusalem at this time.

Have you ever noticed that it's when things look darkest that God acts? I think it's yet another way that He reveals Himself to His creation.

Sometimes we have to reach the end of all our options and plans before God acts; otherwise, we'd try to claim some of the credit for ourselves. It's in our sin nature. But when all our plans have failed and God comes through, there's no denying that He worked on our behalf.

This is exactly what happened when Hezekiah refused to surrender to the Assyrian officials in 2 Kings 18 and Isaiah 36. Isaiah 33:10-19 may point to how God delivered Jerusalem from that threat, although it certainly has further reaching applications.

The efforts of man are empty compared to the incomparable power of God (v 11) and the only logical response is to acknowledge God for who He is (v 13).

I associate the "consuming fire" of verse 14 with God, for God calls Himself a consuming fire (Deuteronomy 4:24). Sinners certainly can't dwell with Him, but verse 15 tells us who can: those who walk righteously, speak what is right, reject dishonest gain, oppose murder, and refuse to consider what is evil. For those people, God will be their refuge and will supply all their needs. They are the ones who will truly see God.

Now, obviously we have no righteousness on our own, but thanks to Jesus and His sacrifice, we can claim the righteousness of Christ (Romans 3:21-26, Philippians 3:9).

Verses 20-22 describe a time of peace for Jerusalem. I feel like this is a reference to the future reign of Christ. While there were temporary times of peace during Jerusalem's history, that city has seen very little peace over the years. Yet a day will come when God Himself will reign there and the city will be secure and at rest.

Verse 23 feels a little out of place here, doesn't it? My best guess is that it refers to the enemies of God – perhaps specifically Assyria or Babylon, in this instance – that they are like a ship dead in the water, unable to defend themselves or flee from the Lord, and that even the weakest of the Lord's people will overcome (plunder) them.

This chapter ends with man's greatest need, a need only the Lord can provide: forgiveness of sins.

It's interesting that the idea of being "ill" is tied to our need for forgiveness. Sin is a wasting, spiritual disease from which there is only one cure: the blood of Christ. Forgiveness is found in no other person than Jesus.

Isaiah 34-35

1. From these chapters, what impresses, stands out, or convicts you?

2. Isaiah 34:1-7
   a. Why do you think God called all the nations and peoples to attention in verse 1?

   b. Do you think Edom is the only nation facing judgment here?

   c. Why do you think God singled out Edom?

   d. What significance do you find in the mention of a sacrifice (v 6)?

3. Isaiah 34:8-17
   a. Why was God's judgment upon these people?

b. The text lists very specific animals that will dwell where cities used to exist. What significance do you find in the animals that are listed?

c. What does God's care for these wild animals tell you about His nature?

d. How do verses 16-17 encourage or give you hope?

4. Isaiah 35:1-7
   a. What differences would the Lord's glory bring about on the people and the land?

   b. How could we look to Jesus as the ultimate fulfillment of this prophecy?

5. Isaiah 35:8-10
   a. What literal interpretations could be made for this passage? In what ways might it be figurative?

   b. What about the road or highway is most significant to you personally? Why?

Chapters 34-35 – Thoughts and Considerations

What a contrast between these two chapters! I grouped them together because both are relatively short and to highlight the chasm between those under judgment versus those under grace.

Chapter 34 is very sobering and has some vivid, disturbing images.

For most of us, the idea of this kind of rampant bloodshed and death is completely foreign; we live in a sanitized society where we see these kinds of things in movies, but have no real-life connections to them.

For the people of Isaiah's time, however, these images would have been all too real. They would have no trouble visualizing this prophecy.

The level of judgment here makes me think this prophecy points more to end times than to a specific nation or historic event. Certainly there have been nations and peoples that God has judged firmly, some that have been erased from existence, but I suspect a future fulfillment is still coming in regard to this passage.

While Edom is singled out here and did experience God's judgment, I believe it is used mostly symbolically to represent all who oppose God's people.

Perhaps Edom was chosen specifically because the Edomites descended from Esau, Jacob's brother. With the strong familial connections, the Edomites and Israelites should have been allies, yet throughout the Bible we see the Edomites at odds with the Israelites (Numbers 20, 1 Samuel 14:47, 2 Samuel 8:11-13, 2 Kings 8:20-21, Ezekiel 25:12, Ezekiel 35, Ezekiel 36:5, Amos 1:11-12, Obadiah).

The language in verse 6 is interesting. It speaks of sacrifices, something that would have been quite familiar to Isaiah's original audience.

Scripture makes it clear that the penalty for sin is death (Romans 6:23). We know God is very intentional with the things He says in His word. Perhaps the reference to God's enemies being sacrificed pointed to the fact that their sins had not been atoned for, so the guilt of their sin rested solely upon themselves.

I see this verse as pointing us to the cross and Jesus' sacrifice for us. There are two options for sacrifices: Jesus or us. If we reject Jesus' sacrifice on our behalf, the only option left for us is what is described in these verses.

The wrath God pours out on the people is not without cause. Verse 8 tells us that it is for Zion's sake that He takes retribution. Once again, God defends His people.

I was struck by the specific birds mentioned in verse 11. I'm sure there's a deep significance to the ones listed – most translations I looked at indicated that there were issues with translation so we may not know exactly which birds were intended. However in looking at the way it's translated, these birds are all wild, most are either birds of prey or scavengers, and most were considered unclean according to Old Testament tradition.

The details God gives about these wild animals is interesting. Not only will all these birds and desert animals live there, but they will raise their young and call this desolate place their home. Verse 16 goes on to say that none will be missing and all will have a mate.

This is actually really encouraging to me. God cares about the life of each of these animals – animals that *we* really don't care about at all. But God cares. He is concerned with the littlest details of all His creation.

It reminds me of Jesus' words on worry in Matthew 10:31, where Jesus reminds us that we are worth more to God than many sparrows.

Verse 16 is also interesting because it challenges us to search out the things God promises and watch them come to pass. God does not speak idly. What He says will happen will happen, whether it's judgment or blessing.

We should be warned by the promise of judgment and

encouraged by the promise of blessing. God is sovereign over time and all creation.

Chapter 35 picks up right where 34 leaves off, only with a contrast of a lush desert rather than a desolate wasteland. Whereas God's judgment is a fearful thing to those under it, it brings joy to those saved from it for it cleanses the land and highlights the great mercy He has offered to us.

I see these verses as pointing to Jesus. He takes the desert of our lives – sinful, hopeless, and condemned – and brings new life, transforming us into something beautiful and vibrant.

We know that when He came, He opened the eyes of the blind and unplugged the ears of the deaf (v 5), made the lame walk and the mute speak (v 6), and brought living water to our dry and dusty souls (John 4:10-14, 7:38).

The chapter closes with this beautiful picture of people coming to the city of God in safety.

This could point in part to the return from exile, when the people returned with Cyrus' blessing, but there would have still been wicked people and wild animals to threaten them along the way.

It can also point to the cross and the path God has laid for all who choose to take it. Salvation is easy to attain, for God has made a straight path for us to take hold of it.

Yet, again, I don't think we've seen complete fulfillment of this, for there are still evil people who try to trip us up – oftentimes persecuting believers – traps set by demonic forces, and other threats that get us off course.

Personally, I believe we won't see complete fulfillment until Jesus sets up His kingdom on earth and all threats are removed. Only then will we know the absence of evil and perfect safety.

Now we leave the chapters on the judgments of the nations (and we all breathe a sigh of relief!) and move into a few chapters of historic accounts, where we see some of the events we've just read about take place.

Isaiah 36

1. From this chapter, what impresses, stands out, or convicts you?

2. Isaiah 36:1-10
   a. What strategies and arguments did the Assyrians use to try to convince Hezekiah and the people to surrender?

   b. What validity do you see in some of his arguments?

   c. What errors do you see in some of his arguments?

   d. In what current trial are you attempting victory using only human resources and methods?

3. Isaiah 36:11-22
   a. What do you think about the way Hezekiah's officials responded to the Assyrian and his threats?

b. How did the Assyrian commander change his tactics when addressing the more common people?

c. Who were the people being tempted to doubt? How can you relate to this temptation?

d. In what ways did the commander glamorize life under Assyrian rule? Do you think his words were true or would the people have been disappointed had they believed his promises?

e. What false promises of sin are currently in front of you? How does this chapter help you to stand firm?

f. How did the Assyrian commander's words reveal his ignorance of God?

g. In what ways might you be minimizing God's power or comparing Him to lesser things?

Chapter 36 – Thoughts and Considerations

This chapter is absolutely fascinating to me. It's so interesting to examine the tactics the Assyrian commander employed here and to see the way Hezekiah led the people to stand firm and trust God.

Both Biblical and Assyrian records support the theory that this likely occurred somewhere around 701 B.C.

It's interesting that King Hezekiah does not go out in person to meet this Assyrian commander, but sends some of his high-ranking officials to stand for him. I'm not sure why he didn't go personally, although we see that Sennacherib didn't come personally either, so perhaps these kinds of meetings were typically handled by officials rather than the king himself.

Did you notice who was sent? Shebna and Eliakim – we read about both of them back in chapter 22 – and Shebna has been demoted and Eliakim promoted, just as God said.

Verse 2 tells us that this happened by the aqueduct that feeds the upper pool, which may be the same location that Isaiah met with Hezekiah's father Ahaz in chapter 7 (compare with 7:3). If it's the same location, there's a great irony here. Ahaz, an ungodly king, was being encouraged by Isaiah to trust the Lord for protection while Hezekiah, a godly king, was being tempted by the Assyrians to doubt God's ability to save. Ahaz failed to trust God and responded with human "wisdom" while Hezekiah stood firm against the temptation and brought his fears to the Lord (we'll see that next in chapter 37).

The Assyrians use some very persuasive tactics. They highlight how small and unskilled Hezekiah's army was (v 9), the fruitlessness of trusting in Egypt (v 6), that God would not help them because they had insulted God (v 7), and that God Himself had sent them (v 10).

They were right on about 50% of that. Hezekiah's army was small and Egypt wouldn't be any help.

But the Assyrians had a lot of misinformation about God.

For instance, it wasn't God's altars Hezekiah had destroyed, it was the pagan altars (2 Kings 18:4). So not only did Hezekiah *not* insult God with this action, he actually acted in a manner pleasing to the Lord. Also, God had *not* sent them to destroy Judah; in fact, God repeatedly called His people to stand firm against the threats.

But if you put yourself in the shoes of the people in Jerusalem at the time, can you see how these arguments might have sounded persuasive?

It's the reason why we must be so careful with the things we hear and measure it against the truth of what's in God's word. If we don't know the truth, how can we possibly stand against error?

This first set of arguments may have been directed only to Hezekiah's officials (Eliakim, Shebna, and Joah) or it may have been spoken to the general population – Scripture isn't clear. The request of Eliakim, Shebna, and Joah in verse 11 make it seem as though the field commander was speaking loudly enough that the people could hear.

The Assyrian commander not only refuses their request to speak in Aramaic, he seems to shift his focus so that he's speaking directly to the people (vs 12-13).

His next set of arguments focuses on trying to convince the people to doubt Hezekiah, then doubt the Lord. Most of the attack is against Hezekiah directly, proving that this commander had no idea of the power of the Lord. In fact, he clumps the Lord in with the gods of fallen nations (vs 18-20). What he fails to realize is that all those other gods were powerless to save, but the one true God can overcome the strongest army to save His people.

In addition to using fear tactics, the commander also makes some grand promises. He makes Assyrian control sound like a good thing. The people would be able to "eat fruit from your own vine and fig tree and drink water from your own cistern... take you to a land like your own..." (vs 16-17). Had the people surrendered, it's doubtful that things would have gone so well for them, just judging by Assyria's track record.

Think how often sin does this to us. Temptation comes along and says that it won't be so bad.

It's just skimming a little off the top, no biggie.

It's just a small manipulation on your taxes. The government won't even miss it. Besides, they waste taxpayer dollars anyway.

Someone might get hurt if you tell the truth, so that little white lie is actually the right thing to do.

Sure, move in with your significant other. No one saves sex for marriage anymore, anyway.

It's really not a baby until it's born so aborting it is okay. Besides, it's your body.

Do you see how easy it is? Those are only a sampling of the lies that we're told. If you check the Bible, you'll see what God has to say about each of those issues and it's nothing like what our culture says.

Don't measure your decisions against the culture or even the law of the land; measure them against God's word. Many of those things listed above are legal, but that doesn't make them right.

I'm impressed by the people in this passage. They remained silent, even in the face of the commander and his persuasion. It must've been hard. They were aware of the Assyrian army's might. Most of Judah had already fallen at this point (v 1). Now the Assyrian army is camping at their doorstep. I'm sure fear tempted many of them to defect, yet Scripture doesn't record anyone who actually did.

This is a good encouragement to us to stand firm.

Things looked bleak for the people, yet they had their instructions from Hezekiah (who, presumably, received them from God) and they chose to obey. They stood firm, regardless of the reality before their eyes.

Where in your life do you need to close your physical eyes and see with your spiritual ones? Where do you need to claim the promises of God, in spite of the odds stacked against them?

Isaiah 37

1. From this chapter, what impresses, stands out, or convicts you?

2. Isaiah 37:1-7
   a. What does Hezekiah's response to the Assyrian threat reveal about his character?

   b. What does Hezekiah's message to Isaiah reveal about him?

   c. How could God's response encourage you when you face enemies in your own life?

3. Isaiah 37:8-20
   a. Thinking back to the commander's tactics in chapter 36, how is Sennacherib's message more focused?

b. Compare Hezekiah's response in verses 3-4 with his prayer here. What differences in attitude, approach, and perspective do you see?

c. What reason does Hezekiah give for asking God to act and what do you learn from this?

d. In what current trial are you focusing on the problem more than God?

4. Isaiah 37:21-29
a. Of what sins does God accuse Sennacherib?

b. What warnings for your own life do you see in God's message to Sennacherib?

c. How is human pride an insult to God?

5. Isaiah 37:30-38
a. How would the sign given in verse 30 encourage Hezekiah to stand firm?

b. What do you find remarkable about God's message regarding the king of Assyria?

c. What is ironic about Sennacherib's death?

d. In what ways have you witnessed God act mightily on your behalf?

Chapter 37 – Thoughts and Considerations

There's a lot of amazing things that happen in this chapter. I hope you were blessed as you studied it.

One of the biggest things that stood out to me is the change in Hezekiah.

In verses 1-4, he's despondent and sends a delegation to Isaiah to ask for prayer – never a bad thing in the face of a crisis. What really stood out to me about that, though, is the wording used. In verse 4, Hezekiah says "the Lord *your* God" twice – why didn't Hezekiah say "the Lord our God" or "the Lord God"? Why the distance?

Another thing that stood out was that Hezekiah thought that maybe God would act because the Assyrians had dared to defy Him, but we don't see any indication that Hezekiah expected God to act on behalf of His people. In fact, his defeated attitude makes me think that Hezekiah didn't expect God to act period. How could a godly king have such little faith in God?

I think, perhaps, that he was too focused on his circumstances and not focused enough on the One he served.

Can you relate? I know I can.

Whatever the issue was, we see a marked change in Hezekiah later on, after Sennacherib's message arrives. In verse 15, we see that Hezekiah goes to the Lord personally. He addresses God as "Lord Almighty, the God of Israel…"

Do you notice the difference right there? Not only is he acknowledging God as the God of Israel – and, by extension, his God – *he* prayed for the people. He didn't send a delegation to Isaiah, although he might have done that, too, but he personally got on his knees.

Something changed in Hezekiah's perspective.

I think it's likely because he saw God act on his behalf already.

A big challenge in Scripture (even in fiction or literature) is the passage of time. We don't know how much time elapses between verses 1-7 and 8, or between verse 8 and verses 9-13. I tend to think they happened in pretty rapid succession, but I might be wrong.

Regardless, we see that God gives Hezekiah a fairly specific message in verses 6-7. God promises to move against Sennacherib and that Sennacherib would withdraw – all the way to his homeland.

It appears that this begins to happen almost immediately. The commander hears that Sennacherib is fighting elsewhere and leaves Jerusalem to join Sennacherib (v 8).

The mere absence of the enemy must have encouraged Hezekiah!

Perhaps that's why, when Sennacherib sends a message to Hezekiah, Hezekiah's faith seems stronger than it was before. Hezekiah immediately takes his concerns to the Lord.

Sennacherib's message is much more pointed than his commander's message. Perhaps it's because he addresses it to Hezekiah directly; he's not trying to convince the people to revolt against their king, he's merely trying to convince Hezekiah to surrender. There are no promises or challenges. He simply points to history and how no one has been able to stand against him and his army. His primary argument is that God cannot save them.

Hezekiah, however, knows that he serves the one true God, who is able to deliver him from any threat.

There are several points to Hezekiah's prayer that are noteworthy. First he focuses on who God is – that He is Almighty, that He's enthroned between the cherubim, that He's the only God over all the earth, and that He made the heavens and earth.

Next, he talks to God about the problem. I don't detect any panic here, just concern. In fact, there's an implied confidence (at least I think there is) in verses 18-19.

Last, he asks God to act.

What strikes me is that he doesn't ask God to give *him* victory.

He doesn't ask for a detailed strategic plan. He doesn't tell God how to accomplish this task. He just asks God to deliver them. The reason is even more impressive – "so that all the kingdoms of the earth may know that you, Lord, are the only God."

He asks God to act for God's glory. Certainly, God's actions on their behalf would save them from the Assyrians, but Hezekiah's focus is on God. His desire is to see God exalted.

I wonder what might happen in our prayers if we prayed with that same focus.

I love how God sends Isaiah to Hezekiah and reassures him that God not only heard his prayer, but also that God will act.

God exposes Sennacherib's pride. Sennacherib thought he had achieved all these feats by his own power, but God points out that He decreed it long ago (v 26).

The reference to the hook and bit in verse 29 show that God will lead Sennacherib by force.

The sign in verse 30 would have encouraged Hezekiah. God would provide their sustenance for that year and the following one, but in the third year they would be able to grow their own food – symbolizing the freedom to cultivate the land in peace. Farming involves planning for the future, something the people would be able to do again soon.

Following this, God makes an even more remarkable promise. Sennacherib wouldn't attack Jerusalem. God would defend the city before the attack even came.

We see the fulfillment of that promise in the next few verses.

Over the course of one night, God wipes out 185,000 soldiers in the Assyrian army. Scripture doesn't tell us how God did it – just that He did do it.

Tactically, withdrawing was a poor choice for Sennacherib. It was a sign of weakness. It sent a bad message to the nations and could inspire future defiance or rebellion. Yet it's possible that after losing so many soldiers, Sennacherib had no choice but to withdraw. We don't know the size of his army, but that's a lot of trained fighting men to lose!

Ironically, after all his time in battle, Sennacherib is killed in the temple of his god by his own sons. Not only did his impotent god fail to protect him from his enemies, it failed to protect him from his own power-hungry (presumably) flesh and blood.

I see this as a warning to all of us.

If we put our ultimate trust in something or someone other than God, we will fail. It may not happen right away, but Scripture proves time and time again that only God is completely, unfailingly trustworthy. I'm not saying not to trust people, but our primary hope and confidence must be found in the Lord. Only He is worthy.

Isaiah 38-39

1. From these chapters, what impresses, stands out, or convicts you?

2. Isaiah 38:1-8
   a. Do you think God changed His mind or did He always intend to spare Hezekiah's life? Why?

   b. What lesson(s) might God have intended to teach Hezekiah through this trial?

   c. What promises did God give Hezekiah? How did these possibly exceed anything Hezekiah might have asked or expected?

3. Isaiah 38:9-22
   a. What reasons does Hezekiah give for wanting to live and for why God should extend his life?

   b. What does this teach you about the true meaning of life and your purpose in this world?

c. Do you think Hezekiah is blaming God for his troubles in verses 10-15? What attitude do you think he has?

d. What do you learn about Hezekiah from this prayer?

e. How deep is your worship? How honest are your prayers? What thoughts or emotions are you attempting to hide from God?

4. Isaiah 39:1-8
   a. Why was Hezekiah wrong in the way he welcomed the envoys from Babylon?

   b. What do you learn about Hezekiah's attitudes and heart from this passage?

   c. What does this passage teach you about the danger of pride?

d. Do you think Hezekiah learned anything from this encounter? Why or why not?

e. Why do you think this particular story was included here?

Chapters 38-39 – Thoughts and Considerations

These are some interesting chapters, aren't they? Some commentators believe that these events actually occurred before the deliverance in chapters 36-37, citing the promise in 38:6 as proof.

However, this promise could have been a continued reassurance that God would not allow Jerusalem to fall to Assyria. I tend to think that they occurred in the order listed here, for the historical books have these events in this same order (compare 2 Chronicles 32).

Whatever the timing, there are many lessons to learn here.

It's likely that Hezekiah was around 39 years old at this time (compare with age and timeline given in 2 Chronicles 29:1) and possibly had not yet had an heir, which might be the reason for his deep despair at Isaiah's message of death. 39:7 may support this theory as it speaks of descendants that will be born to Hezekiah, although it could look more to grandchildren than his direct children. Also, 2 Chronicles 33:1 said that Manasseh (Hezekiah's son) became king at the young age of 12 and if Hezekiah's life was extended 15 years, then it seems likely that Manasseh was born 3 years after this illness – although the system of reigning as a co-regent, which was common in that society, throws this somewhat into question.

I think God sent this illness to Hezekiah to get his attention and cause him to turn to the Lord and seek God more deeply. After the way God had acted on his behalf with Sennacherib (assuming that God had already delivered Jerusalem at this time), it's possible that Hezekiah might have grown complacent.

I know I've seen this cycle in my own life.

God does something amazing, I'm blown away, then life moves

on and, without a crisis looming, I end up praying less and doing more in my own strength. I'm not saying this is what was going on in Hezekiah's life, but it's a possibility.

Regardless, we see that God answers Hezekiah's prayer. In fact, He gives Hezekiah a firm timeline, as well as a promise of protection, then confirms it with a sign – a shadow moving backwards.

This would be something that only God could do.

If the shadow moved backward, it seems logical that the sun also moved backward (cause and effect). Further, it didn't just move backward some random amount. It was the very precise amount of ten steps. That's a pretty definitive sign!

The healing sparks praise from Hezekiah. He acknowledges that God has all power over life and death. I like the quiet acceptance in verses 15-16. He accepts God's plan, even "finds life" in it.

I mentioned at the beginning of this study that I'm using 2 different translations – NIV and NLT. There's an interesting difference in verse 16 that I'd like to highlight here. The NLT starts off verse 16 this way: "Lord, Your discipline is good, for it leads to life and health." The NIV simply says: "Lord, by such things people live…"

I bring this up because it's possible that God was using this illness as a means of discipline or correction on some sin in Hezekiah's life. However, to automatically assume that this was the case would be a grave error on our part.

Sometimes God does use illness, injury, or hardship as a means of discipline; but other times, these things are nothing more than the consequences of living life in a sin-riddled, fallen world. We can't automatically assume that a cancer diagnosis, sudden loss of a job, car accident, or death of a loved one is God's hand of judgment in our lives. More often than not, I believe these things are just part of life.

However, whenever we face any sort of hardship or struggle, it's always a good idea to do some self-evaluation to see if we're harboring some unconfessed sin. When we witness something like this happening to someone around us, we should be very careful not to judge, as Jesus' disciples did in John 9. Sometimes God allows things so His glory may be revealed through His people.

God's plans often don't look like ours. We can fight and rail and blame God... or we can accept that He is perfect and His ways are always right, even when we don't understand.

In verse 17, Hezekiah says "surely it was for my benefit that I suffered such anguish." It's possible that Hezekiah didn't understand, not even after going through the trial, what the purpose was but he trusted God's plan anyway and clung to what he did understand: God saved him and "put all my (Hezekiah's) sins behind Your (God's) back."

He ends by praising God and declaring God's faithfulness.

Verses 21-22 feel a little out of place. It seems likely that they actually belong between verses 6 and 7. If you compare it with the accounting in 2 Kings 20:4-11, that's where you'll find those verses; also, make note of the wording in Isaiah 38:21 and 22 – it said that Isaiah *had* said and Hezekiah *had* asked – past tense, indicating that this happened earlier. Hezekiah asks for a sign and God gives the sign of the shadow and the stairs.

Chapter 39 follows on the heels of this healing with an envoy from Babylon. Assyria is still the world power at this point, so Babylon is not deemed a threat... although, ironically, Jerusalem falls to Babylon in the future after withstanding Assyria.

That's kind of how sin is.

If there's a specific sin or area in your life in which you feel that you're immune, beware. That kind of attitude usually leads to complacency, which can lead to a fall. We're all susceptible to every kind of sin, so we must be constantly on guard. The enemy of our souls watches for the smallest gap and then moves right in.

This envoy arrives with a gift and Hezekiah welcomes them with open arms, showing them all his treasures.

Scriptures doesn't really say it, but I suspect there was a good deal of pride in Hezekiah's actions. For God to condemn his actions as He does, it seems likely that Hezekiah was "showing off," like a peacock displaying his plumage.

It's possible (likely, even) that Babylon has ulterior motives for this visit.

It seems unlikely that they would travel all that way merely to give Hezekiah the equivalent of a get well soon gift. More likely, they were there for political reasons. Perhaps they wanted to see the size and strength of Hezekiah's kingdom to deem the threat level there. Or perhaps they were attempting to form an alliance with Hezekiah against Assyria.

It's interesting to compare these chapters with the brief account given in 2 Chronicles 32:24-31. We learn that after his healing, Hezekiah became proud and aroused God's anger. He repented and was forgiven. He was also very wealthy. 2 Chronicles 32:31 is very interesting because it specifically states that when the Babylonian envoy arrived, "God withdrew from Hezekiah in order to test him and to see what was really in his heart."

God knows our hearts, so I think these tests are often for our benefit... for they reveal to *us* what is in our hearts. It's often through these tests that we recognize sins of which we were completely unaware before.

Isaiah calls him out on his sin and gives him a prophecy for the future.

I find Hezekiah's response very interesting. He says "the message you have given me from the Lord is good."

If I'd been told that my country, my family, and my treasures were going to be taken captive in the future, I don't know that I would have the same response. Verse 8 reveals that Hezekiah is thinking about the peace he will enjoy in his lifetime. I don't know if he was being selfish or was simply expressing gratitude for God's mercy to him.

Either way, we see that his actions had consequences that stretched far into the future.

Would Babylon have invaded and overcome Jerusalem had Hezekiah acted differently? We'll never know.

Most of us tend to downplay the seriousness of pride, but these chapters show that it is a sin that God deals with firmly. It's no wonder, given that pride often leads to other sins and is a direct affront to God, for it places self on the throne of our lives – which is a spot that should be reserved for God alone.

Where has pride crept into your life? Will you choose to give it over to God now, before He exposes it for all to see?

This concludes the historical portion of the book of Isaiah. Now, we'll move into some of the most beautiful chapters in the book, chapters that focus on the wonder, majesty, and incomparable power of God Himself.

Isaiah 40

1. From this chapter, what impresses, stands out, or convicts you?

2. Isaiah 40:1-11
   a. How does God demonstrate the comfort He promised in verse 1?

   b. How would you summarize the main message of verses 6-8?

   c. What directions or calling do you see in these verses?

   d. What are some practical ways you can apply these callings in your life today?

3. Isaiah 40:12-26
   a. What was Isaiah's (and ultimately God's) purpose in these verses?

b. What things, in which people commonly place their trust, does Isaiah single out?

c. Which of these verses proving the superiority of God is most meaningful to you? Why?

4. Isaiah 40:27-31
   a. What were the people's concerns or complaints in verse 27?

   b. How do the surrounding verses disprove the validity of these claims?

   c. What is the "catch" to receiving strength and power from the Lord?

   d. In what situations have you witnessed or experienced the strength that comes from trusting in God?

   e. Which of your present attitudes or actions show a lack of trust in God?

Chapter 40 – Thoughts and Considerations

This is probably one of my favorite chapters in the Old Testament. Personally, it brings perspective to the "big deals" of everyday life and reminds me just what a "big deal" God truly is.

The chapter starts on an incredibly personal and tender tone. God calls for comfort for "*My* people" and calls Himself "*your* God." In spite of their utter lack of faithfulness, God still claimed them as His own, a promise He extends to each of us today.

Verses 3-5 are largely understood to reference John the Baptist's ministry, which was to point to the Messiah. John called the nation to repentance, thus fulfilling the call to "prepare the way for the Lord." His ministry occurred in the wilderness (desert).

All who truly seek God will find that God Himself will raise up the valley, lower the mountains and hills, and smooth the rough and rugged ground so that they can easily come to God (v 4). Not that life will suddenly be easy – Isaiah and all the prophets could testify otherwise – but God makes the way to know Him easy through simple faith in Jesus.

I see the main point of verses 6-8 as contrasting the faithless and frail nature of mankind with the trustworthy and eternal nature of God.

People are always saying they'll do something and may have the best of intentions, but none of us can keep our word perfectly. Only God can do that. Like grass, people wither and fail but God and His words endure.

Verse 10 talks about God coming with His reward and recompense. I might be wrong, but I've always thought that those terms refer to God's people. When He comes in power, He will bring with Him those He has redeemed. Jesus said that He wouldn't lose even one of those that God has given Him (John 10:28-29,

17:11-12).

If this is a reference to us, what an amazing thing that God would call us His reward!

I love the image of the Shepherd in verse 11. His care for His own is matchless. He holds the young and vulnerable close to His heart; they feel His great love for them and experience the safety only He can provide. Others He gently leads. Our Shepherd knows our needs and responds to us differently, depending upon where we're at on this journey. We can trust Him to lead us in the way He knows is best.

Verses 12-15 have to be some of the most glorious in this whole book. Anytime I start minimizing God in my mind, all I have to do is come here and find this image of just how limitless God is.

Think about the size of the universe – God has measured it with His hand.

What about all the water in the oceans? God has measured those with just the hollow of His hand – not even the whole hand!

He has held all the dust in all the earth in a basket. He has weighed the mountains. He has balanced the hills.

If that doesn't blow your mind, you're not thinking deeply enough.

The rhetorical questions of verses 13-14 should kill any desire we might have to instruct God on what to do next. God doesn't need us and He certainly doesn't need us to give Him instructions or direction.

Following this grand description of God, Scripture launches into the idol making process. Not only does God not need us for instruction, He doesn't need us to "make" Him. By contrast, an idol must be fashioned by human hands. The idol makers use quality materials so that the idol will not rot; they use skilled craftsmen so that the idol won't topple.

When it's worded like that, idols seem pretty absurd, don't they? Yet we all have things that we look to for guidance, people or things we trust more than God.

One of the biggest idols I see in our day is self-sufficiency, followed closely by money. Neither of these things is necessarily bad, for taking care of our own needs is a Biblical principle (1 Timothy 5:8) but they become sin when we trust in them more than God.

God reminds us yet again of His greatness. He created the heavens and brings out all the stars by name. No star is missing from His sight.

Yet Jacob (Israel and Judah) had the nerve to whine that God couldn't see them and didn't care about their cause. If He knows the stars – who are not made in His likeness – by name, how much more does He know each one of us?

The chapter ends with a very familiar passage. God never grows tired and gives strength to the weak. Did you catch our responsibility to claim these promises? We must place our hope in the Lord.

True strength is found in the Lord. He will never let us down.

Isaiah 41

1. From this chapter, what impresses, stands out, or convicts you?

2. Isaiah 41:1-7
   a. What do you learn about the "one from the East" described in these verses?

   b. How did the people respond in light of the impending attacks described in verses 2-4?

3. Isaiah 41:8-16
   a. What attributes of God stand out in these verses?

   b. What are some of the promises God makes to His people here?

   c. In what ways were these promises fulfilled? What has yet to happen?

d. In what trial do you need to surrender your plans to God, take His hand, and rely upon His strength?

4. Isaiah 41:17-20
   a. What spiritual parallels do you see in these verses?

   b. How has God fulfilled these promises in your own life?

5. Isaiah 41:21-29
   a. What evidence did God provide to prove His superiority to idols and false gods?

   b. Why do you think that the one "who chooses you (idols) is detestable" (v 24, NIV)?

   c. In what situation are you looking to someone – or something – other than God for help or guidance?

Chapter 41 – Thoughts and Considerations

The opening of this chapter reminds me of a divine courtroom, with God as the judge rendering His verdict. He calls for silence, then calls forth witnesses to present their case.

The king from the east (v 2) is widely believed to be Cyrus the great, king of Persia, who not only allowed the Jewish exiles to return to Jerusalem, but personally provided many costly provisions for the rebuilding and furnishing of the temple (Ezra 1).

It is also likely that verse 25 refers to Cyrus. Cyrus' military campaigns began north of Judah, so it seems likely that he would have worked his way downward.

These prophecies of Cyrus are remarkable in many ways.

First, Jerusalem didn't fall until around 586 B.C. – almost 100 years after the estimated end of Isaiah's ministry. The exile lasted about 70 years and Cyrus overthrew Babylon around 539 B.C. We don't know exactly when this prophecy was given during Isaiah's ministry, but even a conservative estimate (if we were to place this toward the end of Isaiah's ministry) would put this prophecy at least 142 years before Cyrus was "rightly called to God's service" (41:2) by allowing the exiles to return. Chapter 45 actually calls him by name.

The level of detail here is mind-blowing and should inspire us to believe God's promises, no matter how fantastic or unrealistic they might seem. God has proven countless times throughout history that He is completely trustworthy.

We see in verse 4 that God ordained these things long ago and Cyrus' future military victories come from the hand of God and in His perfect plan.

Verses 5-7 show the response of the nations to this rising power. In their fear, they turn to their idols.

It's probably just me, but I read these verses with a highly sarcastic tone – they encourage each other as they build these useless idols… idols that have to be secured so they won't fall over! If they can't even keep themselves upright, how in the world can they protect anyone?

God singles out His people though, encouraging them to stand firm in their faith in Him. He promises that they'll return to their land (v 9) and that He will strengthen and guide them (v 10).

These same promises are available to us today.

No, most of us haven't been carried off by force to another land where we're forced to work as slaves. Most of us will never experience that fate (hopefully!) but we do often find ourselves in Babylon spiritually.

Sometimes it's by choice, like when we drift away from God and get stuck in sin. Sometimes Babylon is forced upon us, like when we're surrounded by people engaged in all kinds of sin with no regard for the Lord.

These verses serve as our lighthouse in those stormy waters. God Himself says He will call us back, that He has chosen us and will not throw us away, that He is with us, will strengthen us, help us, and uphold us. What an amazing God we have!

God takes these promises even further by telling them that their enemies will be defeated by His hand. He contrasts Israel/Judah's size and power (lowly worm, v 14) with His incomparable strength and ability to save.

I see verses 15-16 as the fulfillment of earlier prophecies to strengthen them (vs 10, 13) as God gives them power to overcome their enemies. Sometimes God acts miraculously on our behalf as He did when He defeated the Egyptian army at the Red Sea (Exodus 14) or with the Assyrian army (Isaiah 37:36-38) but other times He provides what we need to fight the battle He puts in front of us (Joshua 6, among countless others).

Verses 17-20 are beautiful examples of God's care for His own, especially the poor and needy.

I see deep spiritual applications here. Jesus speaks of Himself as the living water and the true satisfaction for thirst (John 4:10-13,

6:35, 7:37-38, Revelation 21:6, 22:17). The Holy Spirit in us is also referred to as living water (John 7:37-39) and brings life to the parched desert of our souls. When we allow God's Spirit to work in and through us, people see the difference, fulfilling the prophecy of Isaiah 41:20.

After telling all He would do, God calls the idols to do the same (vs 21-23). In fact, He calls them to do anything at all to prove themselves, but concludes with the truth that they are utterly worthless (v 24).

Sadly, all who choose idols over God are called detestable and polluted (V 24, NIV/NLT). Idolatrous practices often included sick and wicked rituals, such as child sacrifice and rampant sexual sins, thereby making those involved in such rituals detestable and polluted in the sight of God.

We see that same thing at work today. When people worship the idols of self, pleasure, entertainment, or money, they often "sacrifice" their children by not giving them the attention and instruction that the children need to grow into wise, godly, and responsible adults. Sexual sins are viewed as nothing in this culture where we're taught to do what we want "as long as it's not hurting anyone."

The problem is that Scripture shows us that sin *always* hurts someone. Occasionally it's only the person committing the sin, but most of the time that ripple affect goes further.

God turns from challenging false gods to reminding the people of all He would do. He again promises a leader who would be victorious in battle and would help His people. The chapter ends with the blatant truth that none of the idols could foretell this – or any – event, for they are foolish, worthless, and empty.

They say we are what we eat, but Scripture proves time and again that we are what we worship.

We absorb the qualities of the people we spend the most time with. If we hang out with people who use a lot of bad language, we find it slipping into our thoughts and eventually coming from our mouths. If we spend a lot of time with people who are negative and complaining, we find ourselves being more negative and complaining more. If we spend time with people who are joyful and happy, we tend to be more upbeat ourselves.

The point of all this is that if we worship worthless idols, we'll absorb that same worthlessness. But if we worship all-powerful, almighty God, we begin to absorb His qualities as His Spirit works in us to change us into the image of Christ.

Isn't that what we should all desire most?

Isaiah 42

1. From this chapter, what impresses, stands out, or convicts you?

2. Isaiah 42:1-7
   a. Which of these promises is most precious to you personally? Why?

   b. Why do you think verse 5 was placed here, in the middle of this prophecy about Jesus?

   c. In what ways did Jesus fulfill these promises perfectly?

3. Isaiah 42:8-17
   a. What new things had God declared to the people?

   b. What likely prompted this song of praise?

   c. What do you learn from these verses about times when God is silent?

d. In what ways has God brought sight to your eyes and light to illuminate your darkness?

e. Why would those who trust in idols be turned back in shame?

4. Isaiah 42:18-25
   a. Who is the servant in these verses? What marked differences do you see between this servant and the one referenced in verses 1-7?

   b. How had they proven themselves blind and deaf?

   c. What were the consequences of their continued refusal to listen to God?

   d. How do you see these same things in our culture today?

   e. In what situation are you guilty of the same kind of behavior?

Chapter 42 – Thoughts and Considerations

This chapter requires careful reading so we don't confuse the two very different servants mentioned in it. The chapter opens with this wonderful prophecy about Jesus, God's chosen suffering Servant, but closes with a warning of coming judgment on His rebellious servant Israel.

Hundreds of years before Jesus' birth, these verses give an illustration of His character. Verse 2 says He wouldn't shout, cry out, or raise His voice.

This could have a few interpretations. It could refer to His trial, persecution, and crucifixion, when He didn't defend Himself, nor rail at His abusers.

It could also refer to the humble nature of His ministry.

He didn't draw attention to Himself; in fact, we often see Him slipping away from the crowds (as in John 6:15), usually to pray, rather than riding the wave of their hero-worship or claiming the power that they wanted to give Him – power that was rightfully His anyway. Although He often opposed the Pharisees, He didn't yell at them or get into screaming matches. Instead, He would point out their error and move on. Check out some examples in John 5-10.

Think about how celebrities act today. Many take any opportunity to make their voices heard and will be as loud as they can to get attention.

This is the exact opposite of how Jesus conducted His ministry.

Fame was never His goal. He wanted to bring glory to God by doing God's work, which was providing the salvation for all mankind (John 13:31-32, 17:1-5).

I love that "a bruised reed He will not break, and a smoldering wick He will not snuff out."

God cares about the underdog. Unlike our society, who often

seeks to crush the weak, Jesus seeks out the weak and gently lifts them up.

How often did He purposely go to the outcasts, the sick, or the shunned and offer them what no one else would? He accepted the Samaritan woman at the well (John 4:1-26), even revealing to her in no uncertain terms that He was the Messiah – something He did not do often. He healed the lame man at the pool (John 5:1-11), forgave the adulterous woman (John 8:1-11), healed a leper by touching him (Luke 5:12-14), called a tax collector to be one of His 12 disciples (Luke 5:27-32), healed a crippled woman (Luke 11:10-13), and countless other instances. All throughout the gospels we find Him ministering, often not to the rich and powerful but to those who are desperate and needy.

No matter the opposition He faced, He never faltered (v 4) in His ministry. He spoke the truth, no matter how unpopular. He headed to Jerusalem, even though He knew He was walking to His death (Matthew 20:17-18). He allowed His arrest, even though He had legions of angels at His command (Matthew 26:53). He remained on the cross, even though He had the power to come down at any given time.

Finally, it's in Him and Him alone that we – Christians from all nations – put our hope (v 4).

In case we've forgotten, God reminds us exactly who He is in verse 5, validating the promises He had made and giving His full endorsement of the Messiah He just presented (and continues to present) in the following 2 verses.

In verse 6 we see that Messiah will be the covenant for the people. The beauty of this covenant is that it specifies here that Gentiles will also be included. This new covenant, brought by the Messiah, opens eyes, frees captives, and releases from darkness. Through Christ, we're able to see our sin and our need for salvation, accept freedom from sin and death, and live in the light Jesus alone offers. What a glorious thing!

In the light of these wonderful revelations, the whole earth praises God.

Verses 14-17 show the sovereignty of God's plan. The idea of

God restraining Himself (holding Himself back, v 14) is interesting. To me, it implies a very purposeful – perhaps difficult – deliberate lack of action. It appears that God may be withholding the judgment and wrath that sin deserves.

So if God seems silent – or worse, absent – don't worry. He's still there and will act when the time is right.

The chapter ends with a look at a second servant – Israel – who is blind and deaf. As a nation, they saw God do many, many miraculous things on their behalf, but they refused to see Him for who He truly is. They had God's revelation of Himself, which He continued to give through the prophets, but they refused to listen.

He calls for them to listen (v 23), always looking for those who will turn to Him.

Our culture is guilty of the same things today. We have God's word readily available to us. In many countries, it's perfectly legal and acceptable for us to read it anytime, anywhere. Yet how many people truly take the time to look in God's word? How many take time to pray and get to know God? How many attend one of His truth-speaking churches in an effort to honor Him, grow spiritually, and build up His church?

How many even believe in Him at all?

Can we expect any better results than what we read in these verses? Will you, like Isaiah, choose to be a voice of warning to turn people back to the Lord?

Isaiah 43

1. From this chapter, what impresses, stands out, or convicts you?

2. Isaiah 43:1-7
   a. What promises does God make to His people in these verses?

   b. In what ways have you seen Him keep these same promises to us today?

   c. What do you think is meant by the exchange of other nations/people for Israel in verses 3-4? How might this point to Jesus?

   d. How does verse 7 encourage you? How does it challenge you?

3. Isaiah 43:8-13
   a. How would you tie verse 8 in with the verses preceding and following it?

b. Of what did God call His people to be witnesses?

c. In what specific ways can you be God's witness this week?

4. Isaiah 43:14-21

a. Why do you think God brings up His past miracles in verses 16-17 only to tell the people to forget the past in verse 18?

b. To what new thing do you think verse 19 might refer?

c. What does verse 21 reveal about God's purpose for our lives?

5. Isaiah 43:22-28

a. Do you think God really desired the sacrifices? What did He truly want from His people?

b. What rituals might be taking the place of true worship and devotion in your life?

c. Why do you think the names of God are repeated so frequently throughout this chapter?

Chapter 43 – Thoughts and Considerations

This chapter really should be read back to back with the previous one. Verse 1 begins with "But now…" implying a direct follow-up to something just said. When we look back at the previous chapter, we see that this is in direct response to the judgment God has ordained for His blind and deaf people.

Once again, we see judgment and mercy intertwined.

In the previous chapter, God had just stated that His people were blind and deaf; in 43:1, God calls them to listen, throwing off their former deafness, exchanging their dead ears for ones that hear.

Sin deadens our ears so we can't hear God accurately.

It's not that God can't break through that deafness – He's God and can do anything – but He gives us the choice. As we've previously discussed, when we choose sin over God, God eventually gives us over to the sin we so desire (Romans 1:21-32). Yet even then, He calls us back and will speak to us when we're ready to listen.

I love the assurance in verses 1-7. As sinful as we are, God claims us as His own and defends us. Verses 3-4 talks about God exchanging their lives for the lives of other nations. This might have been literal during those turbulent times. Other nations might have been attacked while Israel/Judah was spared or the other nations might have been attacked more severely while Israel/Judah was less severely besieged.

Ultimately, though, I see it pointing to the cross and the great exchange of our sin for Christ's righteousness (Romans 3:22-26, Philippians 3:9). At the cross, God traded the life of Jesus, His Son, for ours, so that we might receive forgiveness and salvation through

Jesus alone (Acts 10:42-43, 13:38-39, Romans 10:9, Ephesians 1:7).

The prophecies and the people would serve as witnesses to the world that God is the only true God (v 10). The things He declared would come to pass and the complete fulfillment of those prophecies would prove His superiority to all others. No idol or false god could make such a claim, but the one true God has proven and will continue to prove that He alone is mighty and sovereign (vs 8-13).

God reminds them of His glorious deliverance in Israel's past when He freed them from their bondage in Egypt and destroyed the pursuing Egyptian army (vs 14-17). After reminding them of these things, God tells them to forget the past (v 18, NIV), which may seem a bit contradictive at first. But if we look at this verse in the NLT, it provides some insight – "But forget all that – it is nothing compared to what I am going to do."

Yes, God had done amazing things in the past, but better things were in store.

Verses 19-21 speak of God's refreshing and abundant provision. The immediate fulfillment likely pointed to the return from exile and the way God would smooth out the path for their return, providing resources for the temple rebuilding and the support of the most powerful leader (Cyrus) in the world at that time.

But certainly it goes far beyond that. I'm convinced it points to the cross and the new covenant through the blood of Christ. God had set that plan in motion from the beginning of time (Genesis 3:15). Only Jesus can truly bring water in the desert and turn the dry wasteland into a fertile field. He brings refreshment to His chosen people and – because His earthly lineage is from Israel and the disciples were all Israelites – Israel honors God before the whole world (v 21).

Verses 22-24 show the current condition of their souls however, as well as the contrast between what they offer God and what He offers them. He doesn't place heavy burdens on them or weary them with demands (v 23) – unlike many of the false gods they chose to worship, whose worship required human sacrifice –

but instead God was burdened by the weight of their sin and wearied by their faults (v 24).

We know from other Scripture that God doesn't really delight in the sacrifice of animals but in the obedient and repentant hearts of His people (1 Samuel 15:22, Psalm 40:6-8, 51:16-17, Jeremiah 7:22, Micah 6:6-8).

Further, no effort of man or false god can bring redemption. Only God provides forgiveness of sins (v 25).

Again, in verse 26, the verses take on an almost legal tone. God calls them to review the facts and for them to present a defense of their innocence. He then goes on to present His own evidence, that mankind has sinned and rebelled since the very first humans walked the earth (v 27). Lack of repentance brings shame and disgrace to all, even the priests who supposedly followed the Lord.

Throughout this chapter, God repeatedly declares His Name, all He has done, and all He desires to do — in fact, this theme is found in all but a few verses in this chapter.

God is completely faithful. We are the ones who walk away from Him.

If you're feeling the distance, will you stop and examine your heart today? What's keeping you from experiencing the fullness of life that God desires for you?

Isaiah 44

1. From this chapter, what impresses, stands out, or convicts you?

2. Isaiah 44:1-5
   a. What specific promises and reassurances did God offer His people?

   b. Which of these promises do you find particularly comforting in your present circumstances? Why?

3. Isaiah 44:6-11
   a. What evidence does God offer His people to prove His superiority to idols?

   b. What parallels do you see between these idol-makers and our society?

   c. Why would those who make and/or follow idols be shamed?

4. Isaiah 44:12-20
   a. With what arguments does God prove the foolishness of idolatry?

   b. How might the truth of verse 18 apply to the idolater as well as the idol?

   c. In what ways have you witnessed our society displaying the same futility of thought?

   d. Explain verse 20 in your own words.

5. Isaiah 44:21-28
   a. How do verses 21-23 stand in sharp contrast to the way the people had treated the Lord?

   b. What actions would God take on the people's behalf?

   c. In what ways have you witnessed God at work in your life? What brokenness has He restored?

Chapter 44 – Thoughts and Considerations

This chapter, like chapter 43, is really best read in context with the one before it. Chapter 43 ended with Israel's rejection of God and God's resulting discipline, which leads to the blessing at the beginning of this chapter. Although Israel had rejected God, they would return to Him. Blessings would follow as God pours out His Spirit and the people would thrive and boldly claim God as their own.

Did you catch the reference to the inclusion of the Gentiles here? The very end of verse 5 says that some... "will take the name of Israel as their own."

This indicates to me that, although they aren't part of Israel by birth, they will choose to align with the people of God. This reminds me of the many places in the New Testament that speak of being adopted into God's family through the sacrifice of Christ and the indwelling Holy Spirit (John 1:12-13, Romans 8:14-17, 9:24-26, Galatians 3:26-28, 4:4-7, Ephesians 1:4-14).

God again challenges idols and idol worshippers to prove their superiority to Him. Verses 12-20 really highlight the foolishness of idolatry, don't they? In the simplest of terms, they show the great efforts man goes to in order to make an idol, how he slaves over it only to bow before it and ask for help. He makes his god from the same wood that he also burns for warmth and uses to cook food.

Verse 13 is interesting. The NIV says "...he shapes it in human form, human form in all its glory..." which brings to mind Genesis 1:26 where God makes man in God's image. Therefore, Isaiah 44:13 really presents idolatry as a warped or backward view of creation, where man makes a god in his own image instead of acknowledging the true God who made man in His image.

This is one reason why it's so important for us to have an

accurate view of God. If we don't, I believe that we are essentially making God in our own image as we try to make him fit what we want or think He should be.

I love the way this discourse is summed up in the NLT. Verse 19 – "The person who made the idol never stops to reflect, 'Why, it's just a block of wood! I burned half of it for heat and used it to bake my bread and roast my meat. How can the rest of it be a god? Should I bow down and worship a piece of wood?'"

The end of verse 20 concludes it well: "Is this idol that I'm holding in my hand a lie?"

Verse 18 could easily apply to both the idol and the idol maker. Just as the idol is incapable of seeing or thinking, so the idol maker is so deceived by the works of his own hands that he can't see the foolishness of his actions, nor think clearly about the powerlessness of the chunk of wood in his hands.

It's easy to read these verses and laugh at the idiocy of all who would bow down to a piece of wood.

Yet don't we place our trust in the same futile things? A few things that immediately came to my mind are money, power, our own abilities, love, loved ones, the government, our jobs or financial portfolios, or even the church.

Again, none of these things are bad. In fact, most are blessings from God!

But when we trust these things over God, we are no better than the idol makers described in these verses.

None of these things can save us, for salvation comes from the Lord (Psalm 62:1).

Yet God is merciful. He again promises restoration and salvation for His wayward people. In verse 22, He promises that He has paid the price to set them free – something that only happened at the cross, when Jesus bore the weight of our sins upon Himself (1 Peter 2:24).

God's salvation should prompt deep and genuine praise from all, for the Creator is also our Redeemer.

God closes this chapter by again mentioning Cyrus – a man who had not been born yet – as God's chosen instrument for rebuilding both Jerusalem and the temple. It's remarkable that Cyrus, a pagan king, would be chosen by God to be used for His purposes. We'll get into that more in the next chapter.

Isaiah 45

1. From this chapter, what impresses, stands out, or convicts you?

2. Isaiah 45:1-8
   a. What do you find remarkable about these promises God makes to Cyrus?

   b. What reasons does God give for using Cyrus to accomplish His purposes?

   c. How do you sense God working in and/or through you right now?

3. Isaiah 45:9-13
   a. What warnings do you find in these verses?

   b. Do you think these verses are saying it's wrong to question God? Why or why not?

  c. Where might you be guilty of trying to dictate to God what He should or should not do?

  d. What additional facts do you learn about Cyrus from verse 13?

4. Isaiah 45:14-19

  a. To whom do you think verse 14 is directed?

  b. Does your life point others toward God? What changes should you make to do this more effectively?

  c. What might be meant by "You are a God who hides Himself" (NIV) in verse 15?

  d. From these verses, what inspires you to thank or praise God?

5. Isaiah 45:20-25

    a. How do these verses point to events much further out than Israel's return from exile?

    b. To what or whom do you compare God?

Chapter 45 – Thoughts and Considerations

I wonder if Cyrus ever heard of these prophecies. Given that they were recorded so long before his birth, by a foreign nation, during a time of great turbulence, it seems unlikely. Still, a part of me wonders if word ever got back to him that the God of the Israelites had declared over a hundred years prior that he would rise up, have great power and military success, and would allow peoples of many nations to return to their own lands.

There are a few remarkable things worth noting in this chapter.

First, the words "I am the Lord (or God)" appear verbatim a minimum of 5 times in the NIV throughout this chapter (vs 3, 5, 6, 18, 22). "There is no other" also appear verbatim in NIV a minimum of 6 times (vs 5, 6, 14, 18, 21, 22). Any time Scripture repeats something, especially so often in such a small amount of verses, it's worth noting. Perhaps it had to do with Israel's rampant idolatry, but God is emphasizing – in no uncertain terms – that He alone is God. No one and nothing compares to Him.

Also worth noting is the similarities between the way Cyrus is described and what we know to be true about Jesus. It's possible that Cyrus is a very dim representation of Christ – not uncommon in the Old Testament – with the major difference being that Cyrus doesn't know God whereas Jesus is God in the flesh. But if you look at some of the descriptions:

- V 1 – God's anointed
- Vs 2-3 – mighty king with power to subdue and overcome
- V 4 – summoned by name and bestowed a title of honor
- V 5 – strengthened by God
- V 13 – raised up by God in righteousness, ways made straight, rebuilds and offers freedom, not motivated by personal gain

In Christ we find both literal and spiritual fulfillment of every one of these prophecies about Cyrus.

Another thing that is similar between Cyrus and Jesus is that they were both unlikely sources of redemption (from a human perspective). Cyrus was an unlikely source because he was a foreign king who didn't acknowledge God. Jesus was an unlikely source because he was born in the humblest of settings to poor, working class parents, didn't draw attention due to His appearance (Isaiah 53:2), and died a horrible death reserved for the worst of criminals.

What really strikes me is the favor God bestows upon Cyrus who, by God's own declaration, didn't know or acknowledge God (vs 4-5).

The promises God makes to Cyrus are remarkably similar to ones He'd made to His own people, many of which He'd already carried out on multiple occasions in their history. God would go before them (Isaiah 52:12, also when He led them through the desert in the cloud by day and fire by night); leveling mountains, smashing down gates of bronze, and cutting through bars of iron all symbolize removing any barriers or obstacles to victory, something God did for His people countless times during their conquest of the land of Canaan; giving of treasures and riches is also something that God did for His people — both when they left Egypt (for the Egyptians gave them riches when they left) and also as they conquered other nations and triumphed in battle; equipping for battle is also something God did for His people, giving them victory despite incredible odds.

We see that God's reasons for doing all this are also the same — that Cyrus, Israel, and the world would know that He is God. He acts for the sake of His people.

God's fulfillment of His promises should give everyone great hope and encouragement.

That's one reason it's so important for us to share about the times that God has worked miraculously in our lives. Yeah, it can be uncomfortable, but it can also change lives. Most importantly, it's YOUR story, so no one can refute what you say. When you share with someone that God did this or that in your life, they can't tell you He didn't.

So reflect on your own life. Take note of the times that God has promised something then carried it out. Praise Him for times of deliverance or intervention. Then share with someone who needs to hear it. Who knows... God might very well use *your* story to draw that person to Himself.

Verses 9-10 are both laughable and sobering. It's easy to laugh at the idea of a clay pot turning to its creator and asking why it was made as it was. The mental image alone is amusing.

The sobering part comes when we turn that inward.

If you're being honest, how often do you think that God must have made a mistake when He made you as He did? Have you ever thought that you needed to correct God's mistake?

What dangerous ground this is!

God has made every person exactly as He wanted him or her to be (Genesis 1:27, Job 10:8-12, Psalm 139:13-16).

Don't misunderstand me here. It's not bad to seek self-improvement. In fact, it's critical to both physical and spiritual growth.

We should constantly strive to do better, to know more, to grow and develop our skills and abilities. We should absolutely seek to improve our health and grow in wisdom. In fact, I think that when people say "well, God made me this way" they are displaying a very lazy and unmotivated attitude, seeking to avoid responsibility for their actions.

I don't think it's wrong to take your questions and doubts to God. In fact, there are many examples throughout Scripture of people doing just that. The Psalms, especially, are full of them. The difference is in our heart attitude. Do we take these questions to God for direction, understanding, and clarification? Or do we take them in an accusatory tone, expecting God to defend His actions?

Starting at verse 14, the passage speaks of a time when all nations will recognize the people of God as having God's presence with them.

Verse 15 talks about God hiding Himself (NIV). Some translations word it differently, so if yours is one of them, this may not have even thrown you. For example, the NLT says that "You work in mysterious ways."

Still, the reference to God hiding Himself made me think.

A possible meaning for this interpretation might be found in 2 Chronicles 15:2b – "... If you seek Him, He will be found by you, but if you forsake Him, He will reject you forever." Jeremiah 29:13 says "You will seek Me and find Me when you seek Me with all your heart." This implies to me that there is a balance to this though; for those who don't seek God, God won't be found by them, essentially making Him hidden.

But what an encouragement for those of us who do seek Him. He will not be hidden from us, but will be revealed to us. I trust you're in that same category with me since you're taking the time to study His word right now. Know that God is not far from you!

This chapter stresses over and over that God alone is omniscient. He alone declared what would happen and He alone brought it to pass. One day all people will recognize this truth about God.

What a beautiful and glorious day that will be!

Isaiah 46

1. From this chapter, what impresses, stands out, or convicts you?

2. Isaiah 46:1-7
   a. What thoughts come to your mind about the idols referenced in these verses?

   b. What contrasts does the Lord point out between Himself and these idols?

   c. What did these idols really do to and for the people?

3. Isaiah 46:8-13
   a. What did God call His people to remember? Why was this important?

b. What memories should you fix firmly in mind to remind you of God's past faithfulness, mercy, and love?

c. What are your thoughts on the man referenced in verse 11?

d. Given that the people were exiled for around 70 years, what might God mean when He says "My salvation will not be delayed..." (NIV) in verse 13?

e. What is particularly meaningful to you from verses 12-13?

f. In what areas might you be acting stubborn-hearted and far from righteousness?

Chapter 46 – Thoughts and Considerations

After all these chapters about the inferiority of idols, God repeats it yet again. Mankind is slow to learn!

Bel and Nebo were Babylonian gods and, just like all the other gods of all the other nations, they were powerless to uphold Babylon's status or save it from Cyrus and the Persian Empire. They would go into captivity, just like all the gods of the nations before them, for they were not gods at all.

There are some interesting contrasts between God and idols here.

Idols are made by man, but man is made by God. Idols can't answer prayers, but God can. The idols burden the people and must be carried about; God does not burden us – rather, He bears our burdens and carries us (1 Peter 2:24, 5:7).

Idols burdened the people physically, but more than that, they burdened them spiritually. The same is true for us today. Idols are anything that takes God's place in our lives. They distract us from what is really important and, because of their powerlessness, really drag us down.

Idolatry is costly on many levels.

We see here that it was expensive – they had to have the gold or silver, hire craftsmen, and haul the idol around.

But there are other intangible costs involved here, too. They had pinned their hopes to the idol, so when their god let them down, there was loss involved. It also cost them for eternity, for God will not share His glory (Isaiah 42:8, 48:11).

God calls the people to remember all He's done. Can any idol make the same claims that God can?

Further, He tells them what He will do – "summon a bird of prey... a man to fulfill My purpose." This is likely in reference to

Cyrus, for Cyrus came from a far-off land and did what God intended for him to do: free the exiles and provide the means and materials to rebuild Jerusalem and the temple.

All of this would happen in God's timing. When He says His salvation won't be delayed, He means that it will happen at precisely the time He ordains.

Verse 13 could also be a reference to the coming of Jesus, for it certainly applies. God's righteousness came near in the person of Christ and Jesus granted salvation to all who believe.

I love that God's actions are not dependent upon us. God calls them stubborn-hearted and far from His righteousness, yet He would send them His salvation anyway. No act of man can stop God's plans.

Though not expressly stated in Scripture, in my mind this is yet another way that God proves His superiority to idols. He is God and there truly is no other.

Isaiah 47

1. From this chapter, what impresses, stands out, or convicts you?

2. Isaiah 47:1-7
   a. Who is the daughter of the Babylonians? What do you think is the significance of the use of virgin (depending upon your translation) in verse 1?

   b. What are the charges God brings against the Babylonians in these verses?

   c. In what ways does this remind you of our culture today?

   d. What would be some of the consequences for these actions?

   e. What might be some modern correlations that we are witnessing in our nation today?

3. Isaiah 47:8-15

    a. What does Babylon's repeated boast in verses 8 and 10 mean to you?

    b. If Isaiah is speaking to Babylon as a nation, how might the nation become a widow and suffer loss of children?

    c. What do these verses reveal about the source(s) of Babylon's trust?

    d. How has our formerly God-fearing nation fallen into the same trap?

    e. In what ways might you be guilty of the same thing?

Chapter 47 – Thoughts and Considerations

If you want to see prophecy fulfilled, do an online search for pictures of Babylon's ruins. It's shocking. Babylon was once a great city, the center of the world during its day, with hanging gardens that were one of the 7 wonders of the world at that time. Now it's nothing more than rubble in the desert.

What's truly interesting about Babylon is that the Bible refers to it often. In fact, my search results brought up 315 mentions. It's mentioned in both the Old and New Testaments and is used in Revelation to represent wickedness and sin.

For it to be pictured in the end times as the epitome of evil, Babylon must have been very wicked.

Here, we see Babylon's certain destruction.

In the first verse, it is portrayed as a virgin daughter. I don't know if that term is used ironically, although it seems possible. What comes to your mind when you think of a virgin daughter? Young, innocent, protected, cherished, favored?

Babylon was none of those things.

In fact, Babylon was more like a mercenary. Ruthless and violent, verse 6 describes it as merciless and oppressive.

We see in verses 2-3 that Babylon would be subjected to hard labor, stripped of its finery and wealth, and publicly exposed.

God addresses the "why" in verses 6-7. He intended to use them to discipline His rebellious children, but they went too far. This topic could easily delve into the debate between God's will and free will, something I don't understand and have no desire to get into here. Suffice it to say that Babylon would be punished for its ruthlessness toward God's people.

We also see the arrogance of Babylon. It thought it would "reign forever as queen of the world" and had no concern for its actions or the consequences (v 7).

Did you notice the wording used in verses 8 and 10? "I am, and there is none beside me" (NIV). Doesn't that remind you of what God said about Himself? Perhaps this indicates that Babylon thought itself equal to – or maybe even greater than – God. With Scripture, we know this echo is fully intentional.

The mention of widowhood and loss of children might represent that they would have no security, stability, or future.

I was struck by the descriptions of Babylon and how we could easily describe our modern culture using those same terms.

Check this out: did not reflect on your actions or think about the consequences (v 7); pleasure loving, living at ease and feeling secure (v 8); felt secure in wickedness, wisdom and knowledge have led astray (v 10); can't buy their way out, unprepared for catastrophe (v 11); receives bad advice, seeks advice from astrologers and star gazers (v 13).

Scary as it sounds, I see a lot of Babylon in our country today. As a country, we look to leaders who neither know nor fear God, take great pride and security in our status as a world power, and are arrogant – especially of things that the Bible says are wrong. If you doubt me, just take a look at what's coming out of Hollywood and you'll see the way we glorify and boast in our sin.

Even Christians can fall into this trap far too easily. We can place too much trust in ourselves and our abilities, find our security in our jobs and our bank accounts, and compromise the truth of God's word for popular opinion. We might even seek advice from ungodly sources. I've heard Christians say that they read their horoscopes "for fun" – Scripture makes it clear that there's nothing fun about astrology or fortune tellers, but that it's dangerous ground to tread.

Are you seeing some uncomfortable similarities between this description of Babylon and your own life? Don't worry, you're not alone! I found a few things I need to turn from, too.

Isaiah 48

1. From this chapter, what impresses, stands out, or convicts you?

2. Isaiah 48:1-11
   a. What point is being made in verses 1-2?

   b. What reasons does God give for announcing what He will do and telling the people of new things?

   c. In what ways do you give others – or perhaps claim for yourself – credit that is due to God alone?

   d. What new things has God declared to you as you've studied Isaiah?

   e. What do you think is meant by "for My Own Name's sake" in verses 9 and 11?

3. Isaiah 48:12-16

    a. Why do you think God gave this declaration of Himself in verses 12-13?

    b. The man referenced in verses 14-15 is believed to be Cyrus the great. What is remarkable about the message God gives here regarding Cyrus?

    c. What comfort or help do you receive from these verses?

    d. What significance do you find in the inclusion of the message in verse 16?

4. Isaiah 48:16-22

    a. What did the people reap in place of the blessings God mentions in these verses?

b. Where have you traded God's best for the world's mediocrity?

c. Why do you think God reminded them of the miracle of water coming from the rock?

d. In what ways has God provided greatly for you?

Chapter 48 – Thoughts and Considerations

This chapter shifts us from Babylon back to God's chosen people – the people of Judah, specifically.

Verses 1-2 don't paint a pretty picture of the people. The people were living a lie; they called themselves God's people, but their lives didn't line up with their words. I'm guessing they claimed God when it was convenient or when it benefited them to do so, then lived as they pleased the rest of the time. It seems likely that they thought their heritage and status as God's people would be enough to save them, but we know from history that this isn't true. Jesus said that God can raise up children from stones (Matthew 3:9, Luke 3:8).

Does that attitude sound familiar? I feel like I see that in our culture and – dare I say – in our churches a lot these days. Have you ever heard someone say that they're a Christian because they were raised in the church or because their parents are Christians?

How about Christians who claim the name of God when it's convenient but don't live like followers of Christ? Jesus said if we love Him, we will obey Him (John 14:5).

How's your obedience?

Do your actions show the people around you that you belong to Jesus? Do you conduct business transactions with integrity? Do you speak the truth in love? Do you treat others as valued children of the King? Is purity a priority for you?

Do you guard the things that enter your mind so they don't end up coming out of your mouth? The things we see and hear really do matter – what kind of movies do you watch, books do you read, music do you listen to?

Jesus said that "the things that come out of a person's mouth come from the heart, and these defile them" (Matthew 15:18) and

"A good man brings good things out of the good stored up in his heart, and an evil man brings evil things out of the evil stored up in his heart. For the mouth speaks what the heart is full of." (Luke 6:45).

Does your life reflect a joyful and thankful attitude... or are you known as a grumbler and complainer?

Do you stand apart from the world by your lifestyle or do you live like everyone else?

In spite of the people's duplicity of nature and stubborn refusal to acknowledge God (vs 4-5), God promises to tell them new things. He doesn't specify exactly what those new things are; likely, there are many. Every prophecy He made would fall into this category, including prophecies about the exile, Cyrus, their return to the land, and – eventually – Messiah.

Any time the Bible speaks of God doing something new, my mind immediately goes to the new covenant in Christ. Certainly God does many other new things, but that one is kind of the pinnacle of all He's done, for it is the only one that truly gives us right standing with God.

Verses 9-12 speak of God's mercy on sinners and make a really good point worth noting: God's mercy is because of who He is, not because we deserve it.

We don't.

The mercy we experience has nothing to do with us; it's all God. We don't deserve it and can't do anything to earn it. This is really good news for us, because it means we can't do anything to lose it. Since mercy is part of God's character, it's ours, regardless of what we have done or will do. Not that God's mercy gives us permission to sin if we want (Romans 6:1-3), but God will always offer us grace when we turn to Him in genuine repentance (Acts 2:38, 1 John 1:9).

God again promises deliverance for His people (vs 14-15). These verses likely refer primarily to Cyrus – in fact, some translations specifically say Cyrus – although it's not hard to see an application to Jesus, especially if you consider the symbolism of Babylon that we discussed when we looked at chapter 47.

When looking at it in light of Cyrus, it's remarkable to me how God describes this pagan king who has no regard for God. God calls him a "chosen ally", says He has called him, He will bring him, and Cyrus will succeed.

God doesn't only use *His* people to accomplish His purposes; He can and does use those who don't belong to Him. So if you're facing a tough situation with someone in leadership, whether it's someone at work, school, in a business transaction, or maybe even in government, remember that God can use that person to accomplish His perfect plans.

We can rest in that.

We see in verses 17-19 that God doesn't desire trouble for His children. Often, the things that happen to us are the result of God's loving discipline on His rebellious children. There are 2 kinds of Biblical refining – the refining of affliction as described previously in verse 10 and the refining that builds our faith (James 1:2-4).

God's heart is in verse 18.

He desires obedience and rewards it with peace and well-being. Not that life will be perfect, for that James passage above (in addition to many others) promises we will face trials, but He will cover us and give us peace, even in the midst of trials.

After the refining of affliction that His people would face, He would once again lead them out, this time back to their homeland. He promises that He will provide for them (as He did with their ancestors when He brought water from the rock) and will quench their thirst.

There's deep spiritual application here, too. We spend our lives pursuing things that don't satisfy, but God promises that all who come to Him will be satisfied (Matthew 5:6, John 4:13-14, 6:35, 7:37-39).

In contrast, He ends this chapter with a firm warning – the wicked will know no rest.

We find our rest and peace in God alone, although there are plenty of things in this world that vie for His position. You wouldn't put a round plug in a square hole. In the same way, you can't fill a God-shaped hole with world-shaped stuff. Where are you trying to fill that void with something or someone else?

Isaiah 49

1. From this chapter, what impresses, stands out, or convicts you?

2. Isaiah 49:1-7
   a. To whom do you think these verses refer?

   b. What might be the meaning of verse 2?

   c. What does this servant's response (v 4) tell you about him and his ministry?

   d. How could verse 5 encourage you when your efforts seem to be in vain or your plans have failed?

   e. What does the prophecy in verses 6-7 reveal about the servant's future?

3. Isaiah 49:8-21
   a. Do you think the "you" in verses 8-9 is the servant referenced above? Why or why not?

   b. To what event or events might verses 10-13 refer?

   c. Which promises does God offer in response to Zion's complaint (v 14)?

   d. Which of these is the most impactful to you? Why?

   e. What do you think is meant by the reference to ornaments and a bride (v 18)?

   f. What do you think is being said in verse 21?

4. Isaiah 49:22-26
   a. According to these verses, what would be the result of God acting upon His peoples' behalf?

b. How would you interpret the prophecy in verses 22-23?

c. What impact do verses 24-26 have on you personally?

Chapter 49 – Thoughts and Considerations

This chapter opens with a beautiful description of God's "servant." I hope you enjoyed thinking through who the servant might be. I see several good possibilities and this may be another instance where there are multiple partial fulfillments.

Ultimately, I believe it points to Jesus. There are other passages of Isaiah that mention a servant and clearly point to Christ (Isaiah 42:1-4). Also worth noting is that Jesus referred to Himself as a servant (Matthew 20:26-28, Mark 10:43-45) and is referred to in other New Testament passages as God's Servant (Acts 3:13, 26, 4:27, Romans 15:8, Philippians 2:5-8).

This passage could, however, have other interpretations. It may refer in part to Isaiah, for many of the things stated in these verses are certainly true of him. It could also refer to the faithful ones in Israel and Judah.

Certainly both these groups might echo the words of verse 4, that they have "labored in vain; I have spent my strength for nothing at all." Isaiah's ministry and the righteous living of the remnant must have felt pretty worthless to them at the time, as they see no change in the lives of people around them. Christ, too, as the religious leaders, the ones who really should have recognized and acknowledged Him, rejected and killed Him.

In spite of this, the servant in these verses has the proper attitude and perspective. "Yet what is due me is in the Lord's hand, and my reward is with my God."

When we release our expectations and leave the results with God, we find freedom. We don't have to worry about whether or not we're seeing fruit from our labor, for we trust that God is working in unseen ways.

Maybe we'll see the fruit one day, maybe not. The important

thing is to trust God with the outcome.

Verses 6-7 certainly feel bigger than Isaiah or the remnant. While both of these did help restore God's people and bring them back to God, and while both did serve as a light to Gentiles, ultimately Christ is the only one who fulfills this perfectly.

Verse 8 references a "you", which I believe to be a continuation of verses 1-7. Again, these things could find partial fulfillment in Isaiah and God's faithful ones, but I believe find ultimate fulfillment in Jesus. The phrasing that God "will make You to be a covenant for the people…" is especially applicable to Jesus alone; no one else has the ability to be God's covenant. In addition, only Jesus can truly free those in captivity and darkness, although God often uses us, His people, to point others to Jesus.

The promises in verses 9-13 can find limited fulfillment in the return from exile, but only find total fulfillment when we look to the cross. Jesus meets our deepest need and guides us; people from all over have come to Christ, causing rejoicing as God shows His compassion to undeserving sinners.

In the face of such promises, Zion complains that God has forsaken and forgotten her.

To such a claim, God has one thing to say – never!

He uses the illustration of a mother and her newborn baby. No mother (assuming she is in her right mind) could forget her own child, especially one she is holding close ("baby at her breast," v 15). Even if she could, God assures them that He never would.

I love the image of God engraving us on His palms and think of the scars of Christ. He bears those scars out of love for each one of us – in a symbolic sense, you could say that my name, your name, and the names of the whole world are engraved upon His palms.

God uses the illustration of an abundance of children to show them that they will have a rich and full future. They would overflow the land, requiring more space.

Not only would the people return, kings and queens would help them return! What an amazing promise! These rulers would honor God's people (v 23), perhaps because they recognize that God is with them.

The chapter closes with a promise that all who oppose God's people will have to contend with God Himself. God is involved in the life of every person who follows Him.

If that's you, rejoice. God is your protector and defender.

If you're opposing God's people, beware. God actively defends His own.

Isaiah 50

1. From this chapter, what impresses, stands out, or convicts you?

2. Isaiah 50:1-3
   a. Based upon God's responses, what accusations might the people have been making?

   b. How do people today say the same things?

   c. What wonders has God used to convince you of His power and strength?

3. Isaiah 50:4-9
   a. What are some of the ways that Christ fulfilled these prophecies?

   b. How might God use you to sustain the weary around you?

c. What foundational truth(s) would help the Servant during His suffering?

d. How might this same truth help you when you are treated unjustly?

4. Isaiah 50:10-11
   a. How would you interpret the message of these verses?

   b. Who is the one who walks in the dark? What do you think are some possible explanations of the darkness in this instance?

   c. Who is the one who walks in the light? What do you think are some possible explanations of the light in this instance?

Chapter 50 – Thoughts and Considerations

This chapter opens with God responding to questions that the people are evidently asking. Isaiah doesn't give us the questions, although we can make some good assumptions based upon the Lord's responses.

It appears that the people may have been accusing God of sending them away. They may have also doubted His ability to save them.

God addresses both of these falsehoods here.

First, He reminds them that they weren't sent away because He no longer loved them. Nor were they sent to cover a debt (a common reason for slavery in those days).

No, they went into exile because of their own sins.

The next two verses address the Lord's ability to do anything, including save His rebellious people. God controls the earth, heavens, and seas – is anything really too difficult for Him?

Yet we find ourselves acting the same way, don't we?

Often it's less about what we say and more about what our actions reveal. Speaking from my own life, when I try to control everything or think I have to come up with solutions for problems on my own, it reveals a lack of trust in God.

Again, I'm not saying problem solving is bad. But do I involve God in the process? When I'm up against something big, do I trust that He's going to work it all out? Or do I worry and micromanage the issue?

The next set of verses presents another Servant – most likely the Lord Jesus. Again, certain elements could apply to Isaiah, but only Jesus perfectly fulfills them all for only Jesus resolutely did God's will all the time.

When we experience persecution, trouble, or injustice, we can follow the Servant's example and fix our eyes on God.

There are some foundational truths presented here that helped the Servant in His resolve and can help us, too.

First, the Servant knew He was doing God's will (v 7). He trusted that God wouldn't allow Him to be disgraced or ashamed (v 7). He knew His accusers' accusations were false and that they attacked Him without cause (v 8). He also knew God was on His side and justice would one day come upon His enemies (v 9).

This section ends with what I see as the ultimate choice facing every individual when confronted with the person of Jesus Christ. Darkness or light. We all choose one. A non-decision is a decision for darkness; there's no middle ground. You can't hang out in the shadows, dipping your toe in the light now and again, and expect to be saved. You have to be all in.

The test is at the end of verse 10 – if you're in the light, you trust in the Lord and rely on your God.

The alternative is to try to make your own light. Good luck with that. Scripture tells us that Jesus is the light of the world (John 1:4-9, 8:12, 1 John 1:5-10) which means that anything else is darkness.

How's your light? Are you allowing God to lead you? Are you walking in obedience and relying upon Him? Or are you trying to start a spark on your own using two wet twigs and your own ingenuity?

Isaiah 51:1-52:12

1. From these chapters, what impresses, stands out, or convicts you?

2. Isaiah 51:1-8
   a. Why do you think God directed the people to look to the rock, quarry, Abraham, and Sarah (vs 1-2)?

   b. To what event or events might verses 4-5 refer?

   c. What point is God making in verses 6-8?

   d. In what ways are you allowing fear of man or of the future to distract you from God's faithfulness?

3. Isaiah 51:9-16
   a. What reasons are given for the people to trust the Lord?

     b. What promises does God give His people? Which one is most meaningful to you?

     c. What are you doing with the words God has put in your mouth?

4. Isaiah 51:17-23

     a. If "awake, awake!" is a call to action, what might be the action Jerusalem is to take?

     b. Explain the analogy and purpose of verses 18-20.

5. Isaiah 52:1-12

     a. If God Himself was going to free the people, what is the purpose of the instructions given here?

     b. What are some different ways God's name might have been blasphemed? How might you be guilty of doing the same?

c. Over what good news might the people be rejoicing?

d. Why would God tell the people to touch no unclean thing, come out, and be pure? What might you need to remove from your own life to personalize these instructions?

Chapters 51:1-52:12 – Thoughts and Considerations

I know this is a big chunk, but these sections tie together so beautifully. In chapter 51, God calls the people to trust Him to deliver. Then in 52, He tells how the deliverance will come about.

God is always faithful to His promises. The peoples' troubles were because they had rebelled and God had brought these troubles to discipline them – just as He promised He would. Similarly, their redemption would be because God loved them and had promised He would bring them back.

God reminds the people of their heritage and where they came from, drawing attention to the fact that God chose them. He called them. God is always the initiator in our relationship with Him.

God would again choose His people and bless them.

Do you see what goes along with the blessing? God's law is proclaimed, His justice is a light, salvation is on the way, and distant lands look to Him (51:4-5). Maybe you think of the law as restrictive and justice as harsh – here, we see that it isn't, not when it's from God. Man has warped the law and perverted justice, but God's law and justice are perfect and bring great blessing to those who keep them.

We are reminded how temporary this world and everyone in it really are when we look at verses 6-8. God tells us that the skies and earth will disappear and people will die, but He is eternal.

In light of the temporary nature of everything around us, He encourages us to not be concerned about what people think about us, but to cherish His law and know right from wrong.

Not so easy to do, is it?

Most of us are naturally hard-wired to worry about what others think of us. We allow that worry to silence us when we know we should stand up for what's right. We allow it to keep us from declaring the wonder of Jesus. Sometimes we even allow it to keep us from speaking of our faith in Christ. But these people we're so worried about will one day pass on; God's salvation endures forever.

Wake up (or awake) appears twice in the remainder of this chapter – once in regards to God and the second time for Jerusalem (vs 9 and 17). These appear to be calls to action.

Depending upon your translation, verse 9 might call God to awaken and slay "Rahab" – other translations say Egypt. Rahab is used repeatedly in Scripture, drawing on ancient mythology. The Bible uses it to display God's power and superiority. You'll find it in Job 9:13, 26:12, and Psalm 89:10. Isaiah 30:7 specifically ties Rahab to Egypt so possibly some of these other references are using Rahab symbolically for Egypt as well.

We are reminded of all that God has done (vs 9-12), which is contrasted with man's faithlessness toward God (vs 12-13). These verses highlight the foolishness of fearing man and show God's power and authority over creation.

I love verse 16 – that God has put His words in our mouths and hidden us safely in His hand. If we're in His hand, what can harm us? The other side of that is that if He's given us His words, we have a responsibility to speak them. How are you using what He's given to you?

Scripture sometimes refers to experiencing judgment as drinking from a cup of wrath (Job 21:20, Jeremiah 25:15, Revelation 14:10, 16:19). Here we see God taking the cup from Jerusalem and giving it to her enemies. God's judgment was just and timely, but it would end at precisely the right time and God would restore His people, as we see in the next chapter.

Chapter 52 begins with another call to action. God would deliver His people, yes, but the choice to participate was theirs. In fact, many chose to remain in their exile rather than returning to their homeland. It would have been a long journey and they were quite likely comfortable with the life they had built in exile.

God doesn't just call them out, He calls them to leave things behind – the chains of slavery (v 2) and the uncleanness of the land (v 11). In order to follow God fully, we always have to leave behind the dirty things of the world. It includes sin and anything that causes us to sin – for them, it seems likely that it might be the idols of the land.

God lets them know that their exile didn't benefit Him (v 3) and He could free them whenever He chose (inferred by the reference to God not having to redeem them by payment).

There would be great rejoicing when the people left and they wouldn't have to hurry as if their lives were in danger. God would both go before them and come behind them, protecting them on all sides.

Think on your own life. What might God be calling you to leave behind? How has He protected you? In what great deliverance can you rejoice and give thanks today?

Isaiah 52:13-53:12

1. From these chapters, what impresses, stands out, or convicts you?

2. Isaiah 52:13-53:3
   a. What might be some possible explanations of the prophecy of the Servant being raised, lifted up, and highly exalted (52:13, NIV)?

   b. Explain 52:15.

   c. What things are most significant to you from 53:2-3?

   d. In what ways have you hidden your face or not esteemed Christ?

3. Isaiah 53:4-9
   a. What new thoughts or ideas stand out from this passage?

b. What evidence do you see from this passage that confirms that Jesus *willingly* became our sacrifice?

c. What significance do you see about the Servant's attitude (v 7)?

d. How might this passage help you the next time you suffer unjustly?

4. Isaiah 53:10-12
   a. What rewards would belong to the Servant following His obedience?

   b. How does verse 10 contrast sharply with verse 8?

   c. In what ways does the Servant's response to suffering convict or inspire you?

   d. What phrase or idea in these verses is particularly meaningful to you?

Chapters 52:13-53:12 ~ Thoughts and Considerations

These chapters are so familiar that I may not have anything helpful to say. Nevertheless, I'll share some observations God gave me as I studied them.

I don't know what translation you're using, but I especially like 52:13 in the NIV: "See, My Servant will act wisely; He will be raised and lifted up and highly exalted."

It's interesting that Scripture distinctly gives all three – raised, lifted up, highly exalted – that, in the English language, have very similar meanings. I think it's possible that the original text had richer words with more varied meanings. Hebrew and many other languages have words that are far more specific than English words. Still, I think we can learn from this. I wondered if raised wasn't a reference to the resurrection, lifted up a reference to the literal lifting up of the cross or perhaps Jesus' ascension after the resurrection, and highly exalted as His current position, seated at God's right hand.

It seems likely that verse 14 refers to the physical abuse He suffered during His trial and crucifixion, where He was beaten ruthlessly – likely so badly that He was almost unrecognizable to those who knew Him best.

Another interesting thing comes out in verse 15. Again, depending upon your translation, it might say that He will startle many nations or sprinkle them. I think either is rich in meaning.

Startle would be appropriate because the sufferings of Christ are an unexpected way to save the world. It's also startling that He would *choose* to walk that road.

Sprinkle is also appropriate because His blood saves us. If you look at the traditional sacrificial system of the old covenant, there are many instances where they would sprinkle the blood as part of their cleansing ceremony. Christ has figuratively sprinkled His blood over all of us who believe, cleansing us from the sin that so permeates our lives.

The next verses go on to describe the Servant's upbringing, appearance, and life. I truly feel like 53:2 describes Christ spiritually; growing up in the Lord's presence, a tender shoot and root in dry ground.

The image of dry ground is so powerful. The culture was very dry (some might even say dead) spiritually. The Pharisees had turned what should have been a relationship with God into a set of rules and rituals, a burden too heavy for the people to bear (Matthew 23:1-4, Luke 11:46).

I like the truth of verse 2 – that Christ wasn't extraordinarily good looking. People weren't drawn to Him because of His appearance. I see this as yet another way that Jesus identified with us. So often, the gods of this culture are people who possess amazingly good looks. That Jesus didn't look like a movie star makes Him more relatable to plainer people like me. Jesus gets what it's like to be judged by His appearance.

Verse 3 tells how He would be treated by man – despised, rejected, grieved – and verses 4-5 tell how He would treat us and what He would do for us – carry our weaknesses and sorrows, be pierced for our rebellion, crushed for our sins, beaten so we could be whole, whipped so we could be healed.

Verse 6 is the culmination of all this and, really, the gospel message at its core. We strayed and followed our own paths (sin), but God put our sin on Jesus.

The verses that follow talk about some of the sufferings He would endure and how He would endure them. If you keep this in mind when reading the accounts of Jesus' trials and crucifixion (Matthew 26:57-27:61, Mark 14:53-15:47, Luke 23, John 18:12-19:42), it's amazing how closely this prophecy mirrors what truly occurred. From Jesus being silent before His accusers to being unjustly condemned, from being killed as the worst of criminals (also symbolic, since He bore the sins of the whole world) to being buried in a rich man's tomb, this passage is full of details that actually came true. How amazing God is!

Do you notice what this passage doesn't say?

That He was forced to do any of it. In fact, to me the wording implies willingness. Christ knew what awaited Him, yet He did it willingly. The gospels, especially John, drive this truth home quite vividly.

Verses 10-12 reveal why. It was God's plan and Jesus could see the reward: the redemption of mankind. His many descendants and long life (v 10) hint at those He saves and the eternity we'll have with Him. Verse 11 confirms this. Jesus would be satisfied by the results of His work — bearing our sins so we can be counted righteous.

If you ever doubt your worth or value in God's sight, these verses should prove otherwise. Jesus Christ endured the cross, but was satisfied... because of you. You are worth the agony He suffered. He loves you that much.

Isaiah 54

1. From this chapter, what impresses, stands out, or convicts you?

2. Isaiah 54:1-10
   a. In what ways had God's people been like a barren woman?

   b. What might be the reason the reassurances in verse 4 are offered here? Of what might the people have been afraid, ashamed, disgraced, or humiliated?

   c. Why do you think God compared His people to a widow or deserted wife?

   d. What are your thoughts on the lines that speak of God abandoning or hiding from His people?

   e. Do you think the promises of verses 9-10 have seen complete fulfillment? Why or why not?

f. Which of these verses do you need to take to heart today?

3. Isaiah 54:11-17

a. How would God's care for the afflicted city far exceed anything they had previously known?

b. What correlation do you see between being taught by the Lord and having peace?

c. What do these verses reveal about God and His sovereignty?

d. What are some of the trademarks of the heritage God promises His servants?

e. How do these promises strengthen or encourage you?

Chapter 54 – Thoughts and Considerations

This chapter builds upon the previous one in a spiritual sense, but in a literal sense it also looks forward to the return of the people from exile. Since that correlation is pretty obvious in most verses, I'm going to focus more on the spiritual applications of these promises.

These verses mention women a few times – a childless and desolate woman (v 1), widowhood (v 4), and a young wife abandoned by her husband (v 6). When reading things like this, it's critical to remember that in those days, most of the time women had no rights or ability to provide for themselves (unless you count prostitution).

A woman's value in that society was seen in her ability to be a good wife and mother. So for a woman to be barren was a huge disgrace (Luke 1:25). To be a widow was to be reliant upon someone else to meet your needs; as a result they were often poor and in need.

Perhaps the worst was to be the young wife abandoned by her husband. We don't fully appreciate the stigma of it these days – of course, the wife would have our sympathy and we'd be cursing her louse of a husband! – but in those days it implied that the wife was lacking in some way. The same thing could be said of women who were divorced – socially, they would have been looked down upon. This passage promises abundance and joy for all of these "women."

If we read this chapter with the previous chapter in mind, we can see that the redemption of our souls brings great joy and rejoicing, filling our houses (souls) with an abundance that far exceeds that of the people who seem to have everything we don't.

The descendants of Jesus (the redeemed) will be vast and numerous, flowing into all nations. The reference to settling there (v 3) could be taken to mean that the redeemed will live among nonbelievers – which means we have unending opportunities to impact the people around us. Does your lifestyle point people to God? Or do you live like everyone else?

Verse 4 is beautiful, regardless of how you view it, whether historically or spiritually. God makes all things new. We don't have to fear, for God takes away our shame and disgrace.

Verse 7 speaks of when our sins are upon us (or when Israel and Judah went into captivity, taken in the historical sense).

God can't tolerate sin because He is perfectly holy, so when our sin is on us, it's so vile that He has to turn away. It's what He did at the cross and why Jesus cried out asking why God had forsaken Him (Matthew 27:46, Mark 15:34). But that turning away is temporary; when Jesus finished the work of redemption, God raised Him from the dead, proving that God had not abandoned Him (Psalm 16:10). Similarly, when we confess our sins, God turns to us in compassion and forgives our sins (1 John 1:9).

Verses 9-10 promise full restoration. While we've seen this through our redemption in Christ, I believe a fuller, richer fulfillment is still coming. When Jesus reigns on earth and the world is absent of sin, I think that verse will find complete fulfillment (check out Revelation 20-22 for more on that). What a glorious thing that will be!

I love the free upgrade God promises in verses 11-12. Think of it this way: it would be like someone taking your thirty-year-old beater car that barely runs and swapping it out for a new, luxury model that always runs smoothly. God would take the old battered things of our lives (or the city, taken literally) and replace it with something superior and far more beautiful.

Did you notice the connection between God's teaching and peace (v 13)? When we listen to God and allow Him to lead us, He promises us peace. Not necessarily the absence of storms, although one day we'll have that, too, but true peace that reaches to the core of who we are. He also ties peace to being governed by One who is just and fair (v 14).

Our world views God's justice in a negative light, but Scripture repeatedly looks at it favorably. God's justice brings peace, for it means that all is right with the world.

He ends this chapter by telling them that they won't even need weapons, for God Himself will vindicate them.

Taken spiritually, we can see the obvious application of our need to remain under God's instruction and leading. But I think there's also a call to an absence of fear here. God can do all things. He is far more powerful than any enemy, authority, sin, or trial. If we place our trust fully in God and His sovereign control, we don't need to live our lives in fear.

Isaiah 55

1. From this chapter, what impresses, stands out, or convicts you?

2. Isaiah 55:1-5
   a. Why do you think the people are being told to buy that which is evidently freely given?

   b. What spiritual applications do you draw from verses 1-2?

   c. In what ways are you working for what does not satisfy?

   d. Do you think verses 3-4 refer only to David? Why or why not?

   e. Who might be the "you" to which verse 5 refers?

3. Isaiah 55:6-13
   a. What warning do you see in verse 6?

   b. What comfort do you find in these verses?

   c. How is verse 10 a beautiful example of what God's word
      does for the human soul?

   d. What do you think brings about the joy, peace, and
      fruitfulness witnessed in verses 12-13?

   e. Which of these verses seems most applicable to you
      personally right now? Why?

Chapter 55 – Thoughts and Considerations

This beautiful chapter uses something we understand well to teach us deep spiritual truths. It begins with an invitation to those who "are thirsty" and "have no money" to "buy wine and milk without cost."

How can someone buy what is free?

Buying implies investment. We buy things of value and usually value what we buy or we wouldn't buy it. Even things that aren't exciting – like soap or toilet paper – are things that are important enough to us that we're willing to part with our money to own them.

I see God's invitation to "buy" as a call for the people to really grab hold of what He offers. He doesn't want their half-hearted worship; He wants their whole hearts. He longs to meet their needs and doesn't want them to casually take what He offers when it is convenient, but to really invest themselves in Him.

He goes beyond just offering "water, wine, and milk" to them; He promises them the very best (v 2). He challenges them to stop wasting their energy and resources on things that don't meet their needs or satisfy them.

Did you notice how they get the "richest of fare?"

By listening. In verses 2-3, they are called to listen (in various terms) multiple times.

So often, the gifts of God can't be bought. Grace is a prime example. We can't earn our salvation. We can never do enough good deeds to measure up to God's holy standard. All we can do is accept that truth and accept Christ as Savior.

While we can't buy or earn our salvation, God does ask something from us in return – belief (John 6:29).

We all allow substitutes in our lives from time to time. We

chase things that don't satisfy, things like money, love, acceptance from others, a bigger home, a better job, a fancier car. We think that if we just lost a little weight, had a nicer wardrobe, or could own the latest gadget, our lives would be richer and fuller. If only your team would win the big game, or your favorite band would stop by your city on their world tour, or you could take that Caribbean cruise you've always wanted, maybe then your life would be more fulfilling.

Scripture tells us that isn't true.

We delight in the richest of fare only when we listen to the Lord. Peter got it, for in John 6:68b he said to Jesus "You have the words of eternal life." Jesus Himself said "My food... is to do the will of Him who sent Me and to finish His work" (John 4:34).

We find true satisfaction in God alone.

God brings up His covenant with His people, specifically mentioning David. It's possible that this has multiple meanings; it could literally mean David, it could reflect the nation of Israel as a whole, or it could reference Jesus. Maybe even a little of all 3.

Did you catch the sobering warning in verse 6?

We're to seek God while He can be found and while He is near... meaning He won't always be found, nor will He always be near. Those who fail to repent will one day run out of chances. Salvation can't be postponed, for none of us know the quantity of our days. Today might be the last one.

Judgment, while often delayed due to God's mercy and desire for all to repent (v 7), will come one day. Will you be cloaked in Christ's righteousness or shrouded in your own sin? There is no other choice.

Verses 8-9 are likely familiar to you. They're quoted often – and for good reason. We need that constant reminder that God's ways don't mirror ours and they are far superior, for He sees the big picture, not just the here and now.

It's interesting that He uses the heavens and the earth as comparison points. The heavens are God's home and we are all stuck here on earth – a good illustration, perhaps, of the vast chasm between God's ways and our ways. In addition, think about the different vantage points. When you're standing on the ground, say in the middle of a field, you can see very little of the world around you. But what if you were in a low-flying airplane above the field? You'd be able to see so much more!

It's the same with God. We see what's immediately in front of us (sometimes we don't even see that clearly!) while God sees the past, present, and future.

Verses 10-11 are some of my favorites.

God's word never fails to accomplish God's purpose. Have you ever talked to someone about God or His truth, only to have them brush you off or, worse, mock you? Maybe they even cut you out of their lives.

These verses remind us to never underestimate the power of God's word.

We may not see the fruit immediately – in fact, we may never see it – but that doesn't mean that it hasn't accomplished His purposes. It could later bloom and flourish in that person's life in ways we can't even imagine.

When God's word takes root in our lives, flourishes, and produces fruit, it brings the blessings of verses 12-13. These verses promise joy, peace, and prosperity, but not necessarily as the world views them. We can have joy in the midst of great trials because the Spirit of God lives in us. We can have peace because we are justified in God's sight. And we can have prosperity because we are co-heirs with Christ (Romans 8:17) and will enjoy eternal blessings beyond value.

This chapter calls us to come to God, drink richly of His generous salvation, and let His word and work be accomplished in and through us.

Isaiah 56

1. From this chapter, what impresses, stands out, or convicts you?

2. Isaiah 56:1-8
   a. What is to be our response to God for bringing salvation near?

   b. What do you think keeping the Sabbath involves?

   c. Explain the blessings promised to the eunuch. Why might these be especially meaningful to him?

   d. What blessings are promised to the faithful foreigner?

   e. In what ways have you also participated in these blessings?

3. Isaiah 56:9-12

    a. What are some of the charges against the watchmen?

    b. How have you witnessed these same things in churches today?

    c. Which of these charges is applicable to you personally?

Chapter 56 – Thoughts and Considerations

Can we ever tire of reading of God's blessings?

Here, again, we see God's great promises to His own. I love that His own includes outcasts and those who would be looked down upon by many people.

There's a strong emphasis on the Sabbath in these verses. I don't want to get into what it means to keep the Sabbath holy too much, because there are widely differing interpretations and opinions. I defer to Romans 14:5-6 on this one, where it says that we should not judge others whose viewpoints on the Sabbath do not match our own.

This is one issue that the Pharisees regularly used to condemn Jesus. May we not follow in their footsteps!

Foreigners and eunuchs are singled out in these verses and promised special blessings if they keep the Sabbath holy (I take this to mean setting a day aside to recognize and honor God), do what pleases God, and commit their lives to Him.

Under the old covenant, foreigners and eunuchs were typically excluded from temple worship (Deuteronomy 23:1-8), yet here God invites them in with open arms. He promises them blessings within the walls of His house, something previously unheard of, and will give them a new and everlasting name.

Often when God calls someone in Scripture, a new name is given to that person to mark the turning point in their life. We saw this with Abraham and Sarah, Peter, and Paul, just to name a few. This reminds me of Revelation 2:17, where God promises the faithful in the church at Pergamum that they would receive a new name. God knows each of us so well, that He can give us an eternal name that fits us perfectly.

God promises the eunuchs a memorial and a name better than

children – something I imagine most eunuchs would have loved to have. To the foreigner, God promises belonging and acceptance. What a wonderful thing to someone who always felt like they were on the outside of that society!

I look at this and think how God knows the desires of our hearts. His blessings meet our deepest need (a need we may not even know we have) and enriches the lives of all who accept Him.

The chapter ends by focusing on the worthless leaders of God's people.

It's very interesting to contrast these leaders with the faithful outcasts from verses 1-8. Of all people, these leaders should have been the example. They should have been leading the people in God's ways, watching out for them, guiding and correcting, yet instead they were self-indulgent, blind, ignorant, lazy, indifferent, greedy, and complacent.

The truly scary thing is how often we see this in churches today.

When a church becomes more interested in programs and ministries than people or reaching out, beware. When truth becomes watered down for the sake of political correctness or attendance, consider carefully. And when whole passages of Scripture are thrown out or discredited because it would be considered divisive or offensive, run fast and far – the leadership of such a church is far too similar to the watchmen described in these verses.

Verse 12 is very sobering, for it displays an "it could never happen to me" mindset. These pleasure seeking leaders thought only better things awaited them. They failed to take God or His promises seriously, thus placing themselves under God's just judgment.

How about you? If you're at all like me, you can see areas of your life where you're guilty of some of these same attitudes. Maybe you lack knowledge – and have no desire to have God grow you. Maybe you stay silent when you should speak the truth about Jesus. Maybe you are lazy or complacent. Maybe you're greedy or selfish. Maybe you seek pleasure at any cost.

Whatever it is, forgiveness and mercy are always available. Turn to God. For as we just saw in 55:7b – "Let them turn to the Lord that He may have mercy on them. Yes, turn to God, for He will forgive generously."

Isaiah 57

1. From this chapter, what impresses, stands out, or convicts you?

2. Isaiah 57:1-13
   a. What unusual blessing is promised to the righteous? How does this display God's love and mercy?

   b. What current difficulty in your life might actually be God's blessing in disguise?

   c. How might the people have mocked or sneered at God?

   d. According to these verses, what had the people's idolatry led them to do?

   e. How might paganism or worldly thinking have crept into your home or daily life?

f. What do you think might be meant by "you descended to the grave itself" in verse 9?

g. How would idolatry weary the people?

h. What consequences would the people face because of their idolatry?

i. This passage begins and ends with verses about the righteous. What do you learn from this fact?

3. Isaiah 57:14-21
    a. What might be the obstacles to which verse 14 refers?

    b. What characteristics does God look for in His people?

    c. What evidences of God's great mercy do you see in this passage?

    d. How can you demonstrate gratitude for all God has done for you?

Chapter 57 – Thoughts and Considerations

This chapter presents a stark contrast between the righteous and the wicked and God's dealings with each. The first few verses are actually a little shocking, aren't they? The seemingly premature death of the good and godly occur without notice or fanfare, yet God says He does it to save them from the evil that is coming. When the godly die, they experience true peace, for they go to God's presence.

So why doesn't God do that all the time? Why do Christians suffer? Why does God allow persecution of His church in so many areas of the world?

I don't know. Oftentimes our suffering draws us closer to the Lord. Throughout history, persecution has only grown and strengthened the church.

Sometimes suffering is just the result of living in a fallen, sin-filled world. Just as cancer, if left unchecked, invades the whole body, so sin infects every single human life on this earth.

While I can't answer the why, I do know that we can either choose to let those kinds of questions create doubt in God and His character or we can allow them to prove our faith. A good verse to cling to is one we looked at in chapter 55; that God's ways are not our ways but they are higher and better (vs 8-9).

So when you face a great struggle or difficulty, remember that God has a purpose in it. We may not see His purpose and we may never understand it, but we can trust Him in every situation because of His unchanging character.

The God who sent Jesus to be our sacrifice so we can enjoy a relationship with Him is the same God who will help you through your struggles.

I find that when I fix my eyes on God, my challenges don't seem

as big. They're still there, the pain is still real, and the outcome may
be uncertain, but God is bigger than all of that.

Verse 3 sees an abrupt shift from the godly to the wicked. God
uses some harsh language with them, but perhaps that was the only
way to get through to them. We've had, what, at least 30 chapters
already that highlight the superiority of God? Perhaps their hearts
were so hard that they needed to be startled by God's dealing with
them.

Throughout Scripture, sacred trees and high places (vs 5, 7) are
frequently associated with idolatry and the resulting idolatrous and
wicked practices (Deuteronomy 12:2, 1 Kings 14:23, 2 Kings 16:4,
17:9-11). Prophets also often reference trees and high places in
relation to idolatry (Jeremiah 2:23, 3:6, 3:13, 7:31, 17:2, Ezekiel
6:13, 16:16, 22:9). It's often tied to sexual sin, a common practice in
the worship of false gods and one of the striking differences
between idolatry and worshipping God. Idolatry seeks to satisfy
self, whereas true worship seeks to glorify God.

It's interesting that in verse 8 it speaks of putting pagan
symbols on their doorposts and behind their doors. Deuteronomy
6:9 says "Write them (God's commands) on the doorframes of your
homes and on your gates."

Not only were the people committing idolatry, they were
flaunting it in place of God and His commands.

We see the results of their idolatry. They had insulted and
angered God (vs 4, 6, 11, 13), sacrificed their children (v 5 – often
done by burning them alive, see 2 Kings 7:3 or 2 Chronicles 28:3,
33:6), committed adultery (v 7-8 – could refer to literal adultery or
spiritual, perhaps both), traveled far and descended to the realm of
the dead (v 9, possibly a reference to the occult), and wearied
themselves (v 10).

The question that must be asked here is: what had all this
gained them?

God emphatically says "nothing." The idols are unable to help
them, nor protect them from the righteous judgment of God (vs 12-
13). The horror of the things they had done, especially to their own
children, had been for nothing.

Yet God doesn't end with judgment. Even here, He ends this section with a promise of blessing for those who trust in Him.

God promises restoration and forgiveness for those who are contrite, humble, and repentant (vs 14-15). I love the mercy extended in verse 18 – He sees all the things we do, but He heals, leads, and comforts us in spite of who we are. He alone brings us peace – and not just any peace, abundant peace (v 19). The chapter closes with one final warning to the rebellious and wicked – they will experience no peace. Their lives will be as tumultuous as the restless sea.

This likely isn't meaning literally, because there are many people who don't know or walk with God that have pretty sweet lives... here on earth. Spiritually, however, there is no peace, for they don't know the One who created them. Eternally, they will never experience peace. The only way to have true peace and eternal security is through God – and Jesus, the only way for us to reach God (John 14:6).

I see the warnings in this chapter as God's invitation to choose Him now. Why else would He bother to give us warnings if not to convince us to turn to Him? What might you need to leave behind today to truly follow God?

Isaiah 58

1. From this chapter, what impresses, stands out, or convicts you?

2. Isaiah 58:1-5
   a. Why might Isaiah have been told to shout and raise his voice?

   b. What do you think might have motivated the people to act like they were seeking God?

   c. What evidences are given here that the people weren't genuine in their pursuit of God?

   d. How do we fall into the same traps today?

3. Isaiah 58:6-12
   a. What behaviors did God desire to see from His people?

b. How would you interpret each of the promises given for those who do right?

c. What are some ways we oppress or enslave people today?

d. Do you think these verses promise that everything in people's lives would be perfect if they obeyed? Why or why not?

e. How might these verses have challenged or encouraged the people during the years of upcoming exile?

4. Isaiah 58:13-14
   a. Why do you think these two verses about the Sabbath are placed with this passage about fasting?

   b. What are some ways we can honor the Sabbath today?

   c. How would you summarize the theme of this chapter?

Chapter 58 – Thoughts and Considerations

This chapter addresses one of the core problems of the people of Isaiah's day... and, dare I say, a major issue in the church today. Superficial religion. We're so good at saying and doing all the right things (on the surface, anyway), but God cares about our hearts.

I see the call to shout and "raise your voice" in verse 1 as a wake-up call. God was telling Isaiah to be loud, make some noise, make sure His people could hear what He was saying (whether or not they would choose to listen is another matter).

The people appeared to be doing all the "right" things. They'd go to the temple. They would act interested in learning about God. They'd put on a righteous front, even going so far as to fast.

But it was all for show. The verses that follow show what was in their hearts.

They would fast – something that was designed to help them seek God on a deeper level – and simultaneously mistreat their workers and fight with each other.

Maybe they were fasting as a way to manipulate God.

Have you ever done that? It might have sounded something like this: "God, if you'll just do (insert request here), I'll go to church every Sunday / donate money to the poor / volunteer / read my Bible..." I think most of us have been there. It might have also been less blatant. It might've been nothing more than a thought that if they fasted, God would be so impressed that He'd give them whatever they wanted.

The Bible shows us that this is not the God we serve.

We should seek Him, do His will, and obey out of love and commitment to Him, not to try to get what we want. True, sometimes He does give us what we want, like any loving Father does for His children, but there's no guarantee.

Are you willing to obey, even if it doesn't "profit" you personally? Your reward may not come while you're in this earthly body; it may be an eternal reward that you won't see until the next life.

God tells us what He truly wants from us in verses 6-7: to seek justice, free the oppressed, remove burdens (one might also conclude to help carry those burdens), feed the hungry, shelter the homeless, clothe the needy, and take care of your relatives.

That last one is interesting to me. I think most of us would do everything we could to meet the needs of our immediate family (excluding certain situations where it would be considered enabling someone or being taken advantage of), but what about extended family? What about church family? We could make the argument that all humans are part of the same family – the human race – so therefore this command is all encompassing. I don't think any of us are off the hook simply because we don't have family or because maybe our families are doing okay and are meeting their own needs without trouble. I think the point of this is to see the needs around us (you really don't even have to look hard), and do what we can to meet them.

Oppression is another topic that comes up frequently in the prophets – twice in these 14 verses alone (3 times if you tie "help those in trouble" in verse 10 to oppression).

Now you might be thinking this one is no biggie; after all, most of us don't have workers for whom we're responsible, nor do we own slaves.

Yet there are ways that all of us tolerate, and perhaps are guilty of, oppression every day. When we pass judgment on another or subject them to stereotypes, that's a form of oppression. When we withhold the love of Christ or lack compassion for someone's hardship, that's a form of oppression. Apathy toward injustice or an unwillingness to act are also ways we're guilty of oppression. When was the last time you were seriously concerned about those imprisoned in human trafficking or the sex trade or workers in sweat shops? These are some of the ugly things we don't like to acknowledge exists, much less look at, but these things are very real and more prevalent than most of us know.

Starting in verse 6, God makes some wonderful promises to those who do as He directs. He promises that salvation will come, their wounds will heal, that He will both lead them and protect them from behind, and that He will answer when they call.

I particularly like verse 10, where He promises that our light will shine out from the darkness. We all want to make a difference in the world, but Scripture highlights that it's impossible to be a light when we're filled with darkness ourselves (Matthew 6:23, Luke 11:34-35).

He ends the chapter by circling back to the Sabbath, highlighting another way (in addition to fasting) in which the people were pretending to honor Him. The Sabbath should have been about God, but the people were making it about them.

How might you be guilty of giving lip service to God? Our heart, words, and actions must line up or we're living a lie.

Remember how Jesus confronted the Pharisees on numerous occasions? It was often to call them out on these very things and the hypocrisy of their own lives. Don't be like them! Jesus applied the prophecy of Isaiah 29:13 to them in Matthew 15:8 and Mark 7:6 when He said "These people honor Me with their lips, but their hearts are far from Me."

Isaiah 59

1. From this chapter, what impresses, stands out, or convicts you?

2. Isaiah 59:1-11
   a. What misconceptions does Isaiah address at the beginning of this chapter?

   b. What are some of the sins that have separated the people from the Lord?

   c. What points are being made with the metaphors in verses 4-6?

   d. What consequences did the people suffer due to their sinful actions?

   e. How is our society reaping some of these same consequences today?

3. Isaiah 59:12-21

   a. What change is seen in these verses?

   b. How did the sins of the people impact their society as a whole?

   c. What attributes of God stand out in this section?

   d. How have you experienced the fullness of God's promise given in verse 21?

   e. What responsibilities do you have in light of God's covenant with you?

Chapter 59 – Thoughts and Considerations

I love how this chapter clearly shows our problem and God's solution. It's a beautiful thing the Lord has done for us!

It appears that maybe the people were complaining that God didn't hear them or couldn't save them, for Isaiah addresses these very issues in the first verse.

When things don't go as we think they should, many are quick to blame God, but the blame never lies with Him. When there's a problem, it's because of sin – ours or someone else's. When our relationship with God feels distant, it's never God's fault. It might be from unconfessed sin in our own lives, or perhaps from a lack of listening for His voice or an absence of prayer, but God isn't the one who moves away – we are.

The metaphors in verses 4-6 are interesting to me.

I look at the idea of conceiving trouble and giving birth to evil (NIV) as saying that their wickedness is at the core of who they are. Their offspring – perhaps symbolic of the things they create and what's important to them – is evil, bringing death as surely as a poisonous snake. The reference to someone eating their eggs (NIV) could be referring to those who participate in the wicked plans of others. The cobwebs that are useless could be symbolic of the worthlessness of the things these people pursue.

This reminds me of the truth that our deeds can't save us, no matter how good they might be (although the references in these verses clearly indicate that the deeds being mentioned here are not good) for all our righteousness is as filthy rags to God (Isaiah 64:6).

These verses are filled with sins for which the people are guilty, sins that are still prevalent today.

Lying is considered acceptable in many instances and many people don't even think twice about saying things that are vulgar or wrong. Sure, most of us aren't guilty of shedding blood... or are we? How about harsh and carelessly spoken words that cut deep? I don't have to tell you that sometimes those wounds can take longer to heal than physical ones.

The results of these things are devastating.

Justice, righteousness, and light are absent in their lives, leaving them to grope along like the blind. Given the great chasm sin causes between us and God it's no wonder that that these things occur, for God can't tolerate sin and God *is* justice, righteousness, and light (Deuteronomy 32:4, Ezra 9:15, Psalm 7:11, 50:6, 71:19, 116:5, Isaiah 30:18, John 8:12, 1 John 1:5, Revelation 21:23).

Verse 12 is a turning point, though. We see that the people finally acknowledge their sin and the trouble it has brought on them. It's then that the Lord acts (vs 15-17) and He does what no one else will – or even can – do.

He achieves salvation for stumbling sinners.

Justice comes in verse 18, but did you notice who is absent from that justice? God's people. It says that He will repay His enemies according to what they have done, but it makes no mention of God meting out that justice on His own people. I'd say that's because the people of God are under his grace, thanks to Jesus' completed work at the cross and their repentance.

The results are dramatic and world-changing. People everywhere will fear the Lord. Surely we haven't seen this day yet!

The chapter ends with a sweet promise to all who repent of their sins. God will make a covenant with us, place His Spirit upon us, and put His words in our mouths. All who trust in the Lord can enjoy these benefits today!

Isaiah 60

1. From this chapter, what impresses, stands out, or convicts you?

2. Isaiah 60:1-9
   a. What might be some possible interpretations of the references to the light and the Lord rising?

   b. Which of your words, attitudes, or actions might be preventing those who are lost from seeing God's light in you?

   c. Who or what will come to the people at this future time?

   d. Why do you think the people would receive these blessings?

3. Isaiah 60:10-15
   a. What promises are made here and what do you learn from each?

b. How would the people's position change as the promises reached fulfillment?

c. In what ways can you relate to their past troubles and future status?

d. Which attribute of God is most striking to you in this passage?

4. Isaiah 60:16-22
   a. What proofs of His sovereignty would God offer His people?

   b. What things have you pursued only to have God replace them with even greater blessings?

   c. What changes will occur when the Lord Himself is their source of light?

   d. How can you display the Lord's splendor to a watching world?

Chapter 60 – Thoughts and Considerations

After all the chapters of judgment and destruction, this chapter is a welcome reprieve. God promises His people blessings beyond compare, the greatest of all being that He would be with them.

There are a lot of references to light in this chapter.

I wonder if this chapter isn't looking forward – in part – to the coming of Christ, perhaps both comings. Jesus said that He is the light of the world (John 8:12, 9:5) and we can certainly see how many of the prophecies contained in this chapter saw fulfillment in Christ. God's glory appeared through Him (v 1), the land was in darkness but the light came (compare John 1:4-9 and Isaiah 9:2), nations and kings came to Christ and continue to come to Him (v 3), even the reference to lifting up your eyes (v 4) could refer to the cross.

These verses saw fulfillment in other ways when the people returned from exile. The people returned from distant lands with wealth and goods, sent by Cyrus himself to rebuild the temple (compare vs 9-10 with Ezra 1).

I think it also points to the future, when Christ will return again in His kingdom, for only then will we know true peace and security (v 11, 18-22).

There are a lot of blessings promised to the people in this chapter. Gathering of their people, homecoming, joy, wealth, livestock, rebuilding of the city, safety and security, lack of opposition, respect from neighbors, upgrade of building materials, no violence, and – best of all – the continual presence of the Lord and righteousness for the people.

Most of these verses are fairly self-explanatory. The reference to the gates always standing open (v 11) means that there would be no one to threaten them, therefore, no reason to lock the gates to keep people out. The level of security promised here would be similar to leaving your front door and windows wide open all the time – day, night, when you're home or when you're gone – with no concern of thieves or vandals coming in. It's similar to the promises made in Revelation 21:25-26.

This verse also contains another reason that the gates would be left open: to make it easy for other nations to bring their wealth to the city. Did you notice that it wasn't just a messenger bringing that wealth? No, the processions from other nations would be led by the kings of those nations.

Verse 12 follows with a warning to those who don't support God's people: they will perish and be completely ruined.

Some may disagree, but I believe this is a literal warning to us today on two levels – one, supporting the church, for the church is the body of Christ (Ephesians 4, 5:23) and the adopted people of God (Romans 8, Ephesians 1:5); and two, supporting Israel, for they are still God's chosen people. Although Israel faces much persecution and opposition today, I believe the day will come when God will avenge His people and all who are not standing with them will face the just wrath of the Lord.

Verse 15 promises a complete turnaround – from hated to respected. I especially love the promises of verse 17. God would give His people an upgrade. He would take the building materials they were using and replace them with something better.

This is what He does for each of us spiritually when we come to Christ. He takes the inferior things from our lives and transforms them, but He also takes the good things and makes them better. If we're walking with Him and allowing His Spirit to change us, He makes us more loving, kinder, more compassionate, and more generous.

Verses 19-20 closely mirror language in Revelation 21:23 and 22:5, and the implications make me think this is referring to eternity, for only then will God Himself truly be our light, abolishing the need for the sun or any other source of light.

When this message was given to the people, they were living in constant fear. War was a reality and many larger, stronger nations had already fallen. Life was very uncertain. Yet God loved them enough to promise that better things were ahead.

The same promises apply to us today. Maybe you're going through a trial right now that threatens to overwhelm you. Maybe you don't think you can stand up under it. Maybe you see no way out of the mess you're in. Cling to the promises of this passage. God is mighty and in control. He has not abandoned you, nor is He blind to your plight.

Rather, He tells each of us to look to what He will do. Our trials are temporary, but the future glory for all who belong to Jesus is eternal.

Isaiah 61

1. From this chapter, what impresses, stands out, or convicts you?

2. Isaiah 61:1-3

   a. Christ quotes the beginning of this passage in Luke 4:18-19. How could this passage apply to both Jesus and Isaiah?

   b. What specific tasks had the Spirit given Jesus (and Isaiah)?

   c. Which of these is particularly meaningful to you? How might God be calling you to do this in your daily life?

   d. What clue is given about why God would do all these things and what do you learn from it?

3. Isaiah 61:4-7

   a. How might these verses apply to people beyond the post-exilic period? How might they apply to people today?

   b. What trades would God make on the people's behalf?

   c. What might be the meaning of the double inheritance promised to the people (v 7)?

   d. How can you live as a priest or minister of God today?

4. Isaiah 61:8-11

   a. Why do you think God speaks of what He loves and hates at the beginning of verse 8?

   b. How does Isaiah's praise to God foreshadow the grace found in Christ's blood?

Chapter 61 – Thoughts and Considerations

This passage starts off with verses that Christ quoted and used to point to Himself (Luke 4:18-19), so we know for a fact that verses 1-3 ultimately point to Jesus. But did you notice how they are also highly applicable to Isaiah himself? That's one thing I love about Scripture – it is so deep and rich that often we can't possibly hope to understand all the applications.

Isaiah had the Spirit of the Lord on Him as he delivered the messages God gave him. Isaiah also proclaimed good news to the poor (to those who were both physically poor and spiritually poor as he called them to repentance), he gave words of comfort for the broken, proclaimed freedom for those in captivity, and prophesied Christ, who would ultimately bring freedom to all who live in darkness. Isaiah proclaimed God's blessings as well as foretelling His judgment.

If you're a Christ-follower, God has placed this same call on your life today. God calls us to do His work, for His glory. Each one of us has been gifted with different abilities. Maybe you're particularly sensitive to the needs of others; use that to reach out and share Christ with them. Maybe you're powerful in speech; use that to tell others about God and how He's working. Maybe you're good at working with your hands; use that to serve others, giving God the glory for what you're able to do.

With God's Spirit living inside us, we all have the ability – through Him – to proclaim freedom for those held captive by sin and to shine light in the darkness around us. In order to truly shine that light, however, we must be bold and we must be sure that there's no sin hampering our witness. For as Christ Himself said "See to it, then, that the light within you is not darkness. Therefore, if your whole body is full of light, and no part of it dark, it will be just as full of light as when a lamp shines its light on you." Luke 11:35-36.

One last note before we move on – the end of verse 3 is critically important. God gives us work to do and special abilities so His splendor can be displayed. These blessings should never be for our glory, but for His.

As we work for Him, it's important to ask ourselves why we're doing it. Is it so people will praise *you*? Or praise *God*?

Verse 7 promises a double portion as the people's inheritance. It's interesting to note that in Isaiah 40:2, the people would receive double for all their sins, yet here the double they would receive is a blessing.

This may refer back to the rights of the firstborn (Deuteronomy 21:7), but God didn't always choose the firstborn. Jacob was the younger sibling, yet God chose him over Esau. Judah wasn't the oldest, yet God chose his tribe for the lineage of Christ. David was the youngest, yet God chose him to be king. The list goes on. God cares more about the heart than birth order, appearance, wealth, status, or power.

God reminds the people of the things He wants from them, perhaps to stand in stark contrast against the empty offerings they had been bringing. He loves justice and hates robbery and wrongdoing. How do your personal values line up with that?

He promises rewards for His people and goes on to outline what that will look like, sparking praise from Isaiah.

I can't help but notice some interesting parallels between Isaiah's praise and the blessings we enjoy in Christ. Because of Christ, we are able to delight in the Lord. Christ's blood has washed our sins and left us clothed in His righteousness, making us as resplendent as the finest bride or groom on their wedding day. The Lord grows within us like a sprout, producing a fruit of righteousness that should flow from us to those around us.

If that isn't cause to praise the Lord, I don't know what is!

Isaiah 62

1. From this chapter, what impresses, stands out, or convicts you?

2. Isaiah 62:1-5
   a. Why do you think the "I" character of verse 1 refuses to be silent? What (implied) difference do his words make?

   b. What blessings awaited Jerusalem in the future?

   c. How are these same blessings applicable to Christians today?

   d. What might be preventing the people around you from seeing Christ's righteousness shining through you?

3. Isaiah 62:6-9
   a. How do verses 6-7 expand the idea presented in verse 1? What lessons do you learn from this?

b. What do the promises of verse 8-9 reveal about the character of God and His desire for His people?

c. In what places has God called or established you as a watchman?

4. Isaiah 62:10-12
   a. What do you think might be the setting or event spoken of in verse 10?

   b. To what do you think "reward and recompense" refer in verse 11?

   c. Which of the new names given in verse 12 touches you most deeply? Why?

Chapter 62 – Thoughts and Considerations

The zeal of the "I" character here – presumably Isaiah, although there's room for speculation – is noteworthy. He refuses to remain silent, for he knows God has given him words to speak. In fact, he says he won't be quiet until he sees what he longs to see: vindication and salvation. That we would all possess that same boldness and stamina with the gospel!

To me, it's implied that his words have the desired result, for the verses that follow speak of vindication and salvation and the blessings those things bring.

God Himself would give them a new name, symbolic of a new identity or a fresh start. We discussed this back in chapter 56, so I won't go into it here, but being given a new name by God is significant.

Here, God would change their name from deserted and desolate to "My delight is in her" and "married." She would finally be fully connected to God in the way He had always desired.

I love that they would be a crown of splendor in the Lord's hand. God can make the plainest, most ordinary person into a sparkling crown that displays His glory and brings Him honor. Wouldn't you love to have that said of you?

What actions might be preventing people from seeing God in you? Selfishness, pride, self-reliance, blatant sin, dishonesty, a lack of love, or… fill in the blank. You know what trips you up.

The watchmen in verse 6 are symbolic of the "I" from verse 1. A watchman's job was to be vigilant and sound the alarm – loud and long – if danger approached.

Again, we talked about this before (chapter 21) so I won't go into it too much here, but know that if you're a Christian, you are a watchman for someone. God is calling you to be on the lookout for dangers and to sound the alarm without ceasing when that danger approaches.

Danger isn't always obvious, though. How do you recognize danger? Through time spent with God in His word and in prayer. How much time do you spend with God each day?

I love the glimpse into God's generous nature (vs 8-9). He wants the best for His children. He wants us to enjoy the fruits of our labor, for our labor to not be in vain. What a great and loving God He is.

The chapter closes with a promise that the people would return. This might point to the return from exile, it might point to the coming of Christ, it might point to His second coming, or possibly all of the above.

Reward and recompense are mentioned here – we looked at this back in chapter 40. The reward and recompense are especially sweet if we look at it in light of Christ's second coming, for it appears that these words are used to describe all who believe in Him. If we tie it to verse 12, it appears that reward and recompense are referring to people, people who are also described as holy and redeemed. That's us!

What does this description do to your view of God and how He sees you? Each person is valuable in His sight. Do you truly believe that? Do you struggle to see yourself that way? Know that Scripture assures us over and over again that God loves us. Christ's death on the cross is proof enough. God sought us out, not because we're so great, but because He is. Let that permeate your mind and transform your life today!

Isaiah 63

1. From this chapter, what impresses, stands out, or convicts you?

2. Isaiah 63:1-6
   a. What might be some options for the time to which this passage refers?

   b. What do you think is meant by the first two lines in verse 5?

   c. How do the graphic visuals in this passage impact or challenge you?

3. Isaiah 63:7-14
   a. Why might the preceding verses have sparked the praise in verse 7?

   b. What were some of the things God had done for His people?

c. Explain verses 9-10.

d. How do people grieve the Holy Spirit today? Where might you be guilty of this same thing?

e. What attitude do you think the people have in verses 11-14?

4. Isaiah 63:15-19
   a. What do you think is meant in verse 16?

   b. Do you think the author/people are blaming God in verse 17?

   c. What point is being made in verses 18-19?

Chapter 63 – Thoughts and Considerations

The next few chapters really tie into each other, but are so long that we'll look at each individually. In chapters 63-64, we see Isaiah, on behalf of the faithful, petitioning God to act and in 65, we see God's response to the pleas of His people.

This chapter starts off with this graphic image of a warrior – whom I take to be Jesus Christ – wearing garments stained red from the blood of His enemies. This image could have a few meanings. It could have symbolized God's deliverance from captivity. It could symbolize the end times when Jesus will crush Satan and his forces once and for all.

In addition, I saw how it could be a symbol of the cross and Jesus' victory over sin and death. The blood reminds us of the old sacrificial system and the necessity of the shedding of blood for the forgiveness of sin (Hebrews 9:22).

There are a few keys points that make me think the warrior is Christ. First, He alone achieved salvation (v 5). No one helped Him and no one else could do it for Him (vs 4-5). He is also the ultimate victor (v 1). If you've read Revelation, you know how the story ends – Jesus wins!

If you're like me, you recoil a bit at this difficult image, but it's important to remember a few key points.

First, in war-ravaged countries, the image of a victorious conqueror stained with the blood of their enemies is cause for celebration. They wouldn't find this image offensive; for them, it would be a sign of triumph. It's only in our modern "sanitized" society that we're so far removed from such images that they disturb us.

More importantly, on a spiritual level, it shows us the seriousness of our sin. Jesus became the ultimate sacrifice for all sin ever committed and shed His blood. Seeing Him as a blood soaked warrior should not be such a stretch for us. Whether it's Jesus as Savior at the cross or Jesus as the conquering King at the end times, the image of His blood-soaked garments shows the severity of sin and drives home that sin has consequences.

For those of us covered by the blood, Jesus took our punishment, but for the unrepentant, a day of bloodshed and wrath is yet to come.

On the heels of this great victory, a song of praise erupts, recalling God's glorious works on their behalf and the people's rebellion and unfaithfulness. It recalls God's choosing of them and His desire for them to faithfully serve Him. He suffered with them, rescued them, and carried them during the hard times, yet they sinned against Him (v 8-10). When they refused His mercy and chose disobedience instead, He showered them in His wholly-deserved justice (v 10).

It appears that it took a taste of justice for the people to remember His previous goodness to them.

How often do we do that? It's so easy to take God for granted, rarely giving Him more than a passing thought until some trial or disaster strikes.

Are you a "hard-times" Christian? Do you just turn to God when you need something? Or do you spend time with Him during good times and bad, building a relationship with God regardless of your circumstances?

The chapter ends with an appeal to God. They acknowledge their condition, who God is, and that they belong to Him.

I love the truth of verse 16. The people feel utterly abandoned, yet they know that God has not abandoned them. Family may turn against us and friends may desert us, but God will never leave us. God is completely trustworthy and utterly faithful.

At first glance, it might appear that the people are blaming God for their condition (v 17), but I don't think that's the case. I think they're simply acknowledging their wandering and that God didn't infringe upon free will to stop them. I think they're also lamenting the loss of close communion with God.

The chapter ends with a look at what has become of God's nation – their enemies have trampled God's holy temple. Yet the people hold out hope, for they know that they alone are God's people, not these foreigners. God has placed His name and His seal upon them and it's on the basis of this truth that they come to God and make their appeal, which we'll look at in chapter 64.

Isaiah 64

1. From this chapter, what impresses, stands out, or convicts you?

2. Isaiah 64:1-7
   a. Why might the people have been asking God to come down and take action?

   b. According to these verses, what qualifications does God look for in His people?

   c. How had the people measured up against these qualifications? What do you learn from this that applies to your current situation?

   d. How might God have hidden His face or turned away from His people? Why did He hide Himself?

e. Do you think God has hidden His face from our nation today? Why or why not?

3. Isaiah 64:8-12

a. What shift in perspective do we see in these verses?

b. What attitude do you think these verses convey?

c. Do you think that God was harsh or punished the people "beyond measure" (v 12, NIV)?

Chapter 64 – Thoughts and Considerations

After clearly laying out his case in chapter 63, Isaiah now makes his petition to the Lord. It can be summed up in one simple word: act!

Isaiah clearly has a big view of God and His power. He knows that when God acts, even the heavens and mountains respond. He knows that when God acts, the nations will take notice, for how can they not notice the awesome and undeniable power of God? Further, there has never been any god who acted on behalf of its people, except the one true God (v 4).

Isaiah may have been asking God to act to stop the Assyrian and/or Babylonian armies from invading and taking the people captive or he may have been asking God for the deliverance from exile that God had promised (on behalf of future generations, since the exile happened almost 100 years after Isaiah's ministry).

Verses 4-5 give us a list of qualifications we should possess in order for God to help us – wait for Him, gladly do right, and remember His ways.

The people had failed miserably in all regards; it's so good we've got those things down, right?

I hope you laughed at that thought, for I know none of us has mastered these things. The beauty of grace is that God acts for us and helps us in spite of our failures.

In fact, verse 6 reminds us of how horribly we've failed God. Even our best actions are like filthy rags to God. We can never be good enough, but that's okay because Jesus gave us His goodness at the cross when He took our sin. It doesn't get any better than that!

The people didn't call on God or seek Him (v 7), so He "hid" from them.

I take that to mean that He backed off. God desires loving

compliance from us; He never forces us to follow or worship Him. So when we start going our own way and turning from Him, He warns and tries to redirect us, but eventually lets us go. We wander and wander until we're so far from Him that we don't know right from wrong.

I feel like we're seeing this more and more in our world today. As always, God preserves a faithful remnant, but the majority are so far from God that they're calling sin acceptable and labeling the things of righteousness as narrow and hateful. I also suspect it will get much, much worse before it gets any better... if it gets any better.

The only way to save our nation is to have a widespread revival and a national returning to God.

Twice in this short section of verses, Isaiah questions whether God will punish "beyond measure." I don't think he's questioning God's justice — and honestly, if we take a serious look at the many, many years that God showed them mercy, we'd have to admit that God was more than merciful and patient with them — rather, I think he's asking God when they have been punished enough. Punishment always feels long and drawn out when we're in the midst of it, but on the outside of it, we can usually acknowledge (when properly administered) that it was fair and just.

Now that Isaiah has acknowledged their sin, he turns his focus upon God, confessing his need and asking for God's help.

Did you notice the tone to his plea? It isn't all self-focused, woe-is-me type stuff. No. He focuses upon how the destruction has impacted God's sacred cities and temple.

The chapter ends with a question — will God hold back and continue to be silent?

How's that for a Biblical cliffhanger?

Isaiah 65

1. From this chapter, what impresses, stands out, or convicts you?

2. Isaiah 65:1-7
   a. To whom do you think these verses are directed?

   b. What sins are mentioned here? What are some modern examples?

   c. In spite of their sins, what attitude did the people display?

   d. How might you be provoking God to His face?

3. Isaiah 65:8-16
   a. What distinguishing characteristics would separate God's servants from those under His wrath?

b. Do you think the contrasts listed in verses 13-16 have come to fruition? Why or why not?

c. What do you think is meant by the promise of God's servants receiving a new name (end of verse 15)?

4. Isaiah 65:17-25
   a. What do you think is meant by the promise of the former things not being remembered?

   b. If there is to be no death in heaven, how would you explain verse 20?

   c. How could you use the promises of verses 21-23 to encourage those who are struggling?

   d. What does verse 24 reveal about how our relationship with God will be changed?

   e. Which of these promises do you find particularly precious?

Chapter 65 ~ Thoughts and Considerations

In the previous chapters, Isaiah called out to God and asked Him to act. Here, God replies.

God's reply proves His mercy, for we deserve nothing from Him, nor does He owe us any explanation. Yet He generously reveals Himself to us, promising blessings and fullness of life.

He starts His reply by reminding us that we didn't choose Him, He chose us. Yes, we choose to respond, but God is always the initiator in man's relationship with Him.

It's a pattern we see throughout the Bible. God called Abraham when Abraham didn't know Him. God chose Joseph to save the known world from famine. God called Moses when Moses was tending livestock in the wilderness. God called David to be the greatest king Israel would know (until Jesus, anyway). God called each of the prophets to their ministry. In the New Testament, Jesus called each of the disciples to be His core group of followers who would evangelize the world. Jesus called Saul/Paul, when he was murdering Christians.

Even today, God calls each one of us. He initiates and we respond.

In spite of His generous love and calling, the people continued in a whole list of sins (given in verses 2-5). It's easy to look at those and distance ourselves, but we're guilty of the same sorts of things today. Let's look at a few of them.

Pursuing their own imaginations (v 2, NIV) doesn't sound so bad, does it? It can be, when those imaginations lead us into sin. We rarely just decide to sin; most of the time it starts in the heart, moves to the head where we think about how "good" the results might be for us or how much pleasure it might bring, then we act upon it. Often our imaginations (thoughts might be an easier word) lead us to do things that God says are wrong.

Our society continually provokes God to His face. The idea of relative truth is just one example. Truth cannot be relative. I can't look at sexual sin and say it's okay for you but wrong for me or vice versa. It's either right for everyone or wrong for everyone. There's no middle ground when it comes to things the Bible clearly outlines as wrong. Yes, there are gray area issues that may be right for one person or wrong for another, but we aren't talking about those.

How can we tell if it's a gray area? Just ask if it can lead to sin. If it does, then we should avoid it, it's that simple.

When we willfully, purposefully sin with no concern for what is right or wrong, we provoke God to His face. In essence, we say we know better than God and challenge Him to do something about it.

We've talked a lot about idolatry, so we won't really get into the sacrifices and burning incense mentioned in verse 3. By now I hope you've recognized some of the potential idols in your own life so you can be on guard against them.

I think the first line of verse 4 where it speaks of sitting among graves and keeping vigil likely refers to consulting the spirit world. Christians have no business consulting mediums or psychics or reading horoscopes, for God has specifically forbidden those things in His word (Leviticus 19:31, 20:6, Deuteronomy 18:10-12). We are to consult and trust God with our future, not look to the stars or spirit world for answers (Isaiah 8:19).

Perhaps the most sobering sin here is found in verse 5, where the people basically say they are too good for God. It's easy to sit in judgment here, but really, how often do we do the same? When we put our agenda or plans ahead of God's, we're saying that our ways are better and that our wants are more important than God's commands or plans.

When we skip church to sleep in or go shopping, or watch the game, we're saying that those things and our selfish desires for them are more important than honoring God for a few hours one day a week.

When we think we're better than another person or pass judgment on someone, we're saying that we are as wise as God, who alone is judge. If you examine your own life, I'm sure you'll join me in recognizing areas where your priorities need to shift. The truly hard part is in shifting them!

God's mercy shines through in the verses that follow. Yes, He promises judgment on the wicked, but He promises that a remnant of faithful ones will remain and that they will be blessed.

It's especially interesting that the Valley of Achor (v 10) is singled out here. Valley of Achor is also called the Valley of Trouble, for it's where Achor and his family were killed after stealing things devoted to the Lord (Joshua 7). Yet Hosea 2:15 promises it will become a door of hope and here we see that God will make it a resting place for herds and for the people who seek Him.

God can take anything, no matter what has happened or the reputation involved, and change it into something to be used for His glory.

This should bring hope to all of us. No matter how much we've screwed up, God can still use us.

When we follow Jesus, He adopts us into His family as His children (John 1:12-13, Galatians 3:26-27, Ephesians 1:4-6, and 1 John 3:1-10). When someone is adopted, they take on the name of the one adopting them and we see that in this passage when God gives us a new name (v 15).

So no matter who you used to be or what you've done, if you have placed your faith in Jesus, know that you are God's child. He's given you His name, His Spirit lives in you, and you don't have to be who you once were. We get a chance to have a do-over every single day! Does it get any better than that?

Now, certainly, we've not seen the promises of verses 13-15 reach complete fulfillment yet, for Christians are persecuted every day and many are in need, but we can look forward to the day when all of God's promises will come to pass. His people will enjoy blessings beyond measure.

When God creates the new heavens and earth, it will be so rich and glorious that no one will remember or long for the old one. Verse 20 talks about death, which will one day be abolished (Revelation 21:4). It's possible this verse refers to a time before the new heavens and earth (perhaps the millennial reign, depending upon how you interpret Scripture, see Revelation 20:1-6), but it might also just be to put into perspective how glorious it will be. Death is an inevitable part of our lives now so we can't imagine life without it. This verse might be here to contrast what we live under now to what we will experience then.

In those days, people will enjoy the full fruits of their labor. The things they work to obtain will be enjoyed by them, unlike during the days of exile when the people would have worked hard (as slaves) for the benefit of their captors.

I think my favorite part is the promise of full communion with God given in verse 24. God will answer before we call.

I see this as a promise that we'll be so close to God that our thoughts will be perfectly attuned to His. The things we ask for will be in accordance with His perfect will so that we won't even need to ask; He will just automatically answer.

Can you imagine? I admit that I struggle to imagine how great it will be, but I look forward to the day when it will be reality.

Isaiah 66

1. From this chapter, what impresses, stands out, or convicts you?

2. Isaiah 66:1-4
   a. Why might God have declared the message of verses 1-2a?

   b. What do you think is meant by the idea of trembling at God's word (verses 2, 5 NIV)?

   c. Why was God not pleased with the people's sacrifices?

   d. What results do you see today when people won't listen when God speaks or answer His call?

3. Isaiah 66:5-16

    a. Why were God's people being mocked (v 5)? What would be the end result of that mistreatment?

    b. What promises are offered through the childbirth and motherhood analogies in verses 7-13?

    c. How does the image of God's wrath impact you?

4. Isaiah 66:17-24

    a. What kind of people are being described in verse 17?

    b. How might the Israelites have struggled with the prophecies given in verses 18-21?

    c. What stands out to you from these verses as particularly meaningful or impressive?

d. What do you think is meant by the prophecy about the worm and unquenchable fire in verse 24?

e. After giving such a beautiful picture of life in the new heavens and new earth, why do you think this book ends on such a dire note?

f. What difference does this passage make in your approach to life today?

Chapter 66 – Thoughts and Considerations

God ends the book of Isaiah with a prophecy of what awaits all mankind, contrasting the future of the unrighteous with that of those who belong to God.

The chapter begins by reminding the people of who God is. He tells them that heaven is His throne and earth is His footstool. The throne is the seat of power; the image of the heavens above and the earth below show that God is ruling over all of creation. He alone has all authority over the earth and everyone on it.

I was also reminded of Psalm 110:1 where God promises to make His enemies a footstool for Jesus' feet (also referenced in Luke 20:43, Acts 2:35, and Hebrews 1:13 and 10:13). Since Scripture tells us that Satan is the prince/ruler of this world (Luke 4:5-6, John 12:31, 14:30), then this verse could also show God's superiority over Satan and all things of the world, for they are under His feet.

The idea of trembling at God's word is an interesting one. I don't think this literally means that we should be terrified of God's word, for there are countless Scripture passages that talk about the word being a delight and joy, food and water for the soul, and like honey. I take it to mean that we should show God and His word proper respect and honor. We should read the Bible, recognizing that it is the authoritative words of the Lord, listen to His words, and obey.

Yes, we should have a healthy fear of God and His words, much as a child has a healthy fear of his or her parents, but God doesn't call us to live in terror, constantly afraid of His wrath falling upon us. In fact, He promises in countless passages – including this one – that good things await those who serve and follow Him.

God gives us several reasons why He might reject the sacrifices we bring: we have chosen our own ways and delight in abominations (v 3), we didn't answer nor listen to the Lord (v 4), and we do evil in God's sight and choose what displeases Him (v 4).

The analogy of childbirth and a mother is an interesting one, yet quite appropriate when you think about it. I take the childbirth analogy to represent the certainty of God's judgment. When a woman goes into labor, you know a baby will be here soon; in the same way, God's judgment will come and often comes swiftly.

It could also reflect the history of the nation of Israel. Following the persecution of the Jews in the holocaust in the 1940s, the nation of Israel was "reborn" in a very short amount of time – you could symbolically say they were reborn in a day, as verse 8 predicts.

For those who know God, His love for and care of them is as sweet and tender as a mother's love for her child. He gives us the best of everything. The world and sin taints the gifts He gives and often mars them, but He always has the best in mind for us and one day it will truly be ours.

Verse 17 likely talks about some of the things people did to "purify" themselves for their idols. It's no coincidence that those things are all things that are unclean according to the Lord.

Verses 18-21 likely would have been difficult for the Israelites, for it promises that God will include other nations among His people. Not only would He include Gentile believers, He would select some to serve Him as "priests and Levites" (v 21). God loves us all and allows us to serve Him in varied ways, regardless of our background or national origin.

Were you surprised at the ending? It's very somber and abrupt. I wonder if that's to drive home the severity of our sin and the consequences for the unrepentant. We all like a happy ending and for those of us who know Jesus, we'll enjoy the happiest ending possible. But it's important to remember that there's another side to that coin. There are those who don't know God and will suffer the worst of eternities possible.

The worm and fire could symbolize the eternal nature of the judgment. There will be no ending, nor will there be any relief.

This should give all of us a sense of urgency for the lost. If we truly believe God and take Him at His word, if we love others and care about their eternal souls, we should be willing to put ourselves out there and tell them of the goodness of God in order that they might have every opportunity to be saved. It's a hard thing, but God calls us to do it. Do you love people enough to risk their displeasure and your reputation? Speak up, for the time might be very short. No one knows the number of their days. They might only have today. I might only have today. You might only have today. Will you make it count for eternity or squander it on yourself?

Acknowledgments

There are so many people who have helped make this book a reality and I thank God for each one.

To my truth-testing readers: Linda, Janet and Del, Lance and Lana, and Judy – thank you. God's word is not to be taken lightly and I am truly grateful for the time you spent reading the rough draft and checking for accuracy and truth.

To the church that supported me in this endeavor and the Sunday school class for whom it was originally intended: thank you. I never imagined God would call me to turn a Sunday school class discussion into something to be published, but He did... and He used you to clean and polish the questions and encourage me in the journey.

To each of you who persevered to the end of the study: you amaze me. I know it wasn't always an easy journey, but God rewards the faithful. May you experience the fullness of His blessings as you walk more closely with Him.

Most of all, I thank the Lord: for preserving His word, for speaking to me, and for using ordinary people like me to do His work. What a wonderful and humbling thing it is. As we saw in the study, God doesn't need us, yet He chooses to use us to accomplish His perfect plans. Thank you, Lord!

A Note from the Author

Thank you for joining me on this adventure through the second longest book of the Bible! I hope God spoke to you as you studied His word and that you can honestly say you are not the same now as you were when you started this journey.

When God first called me to create a study on the book of Isaiah and lead a Sunday school class at my church, I never imagined it turning into what you're now holding in your hands. In fact, a few friends had encouraged me to publish it and I'd told them that I had no intention of doing so. Obviously God had other plans!

There are so many things I've learned from the book of Isaiah and one of the lessons is that God's plans and timing are perfect. I would love to hear some of the lessons you learned as you have studied His word. Feel free to email me at candle.sutton@outlook.com.

For those of you who enjoy my fiction line, never fear! I'm hard at work on my upcoming novel *Silent is the Grave*, book one in The Fallen series, available spring 2018. Don't be surprised if you see some of the same themes we've discussed in this study pop up in that novel!

Would you like to be notified about new releases? How about receiving a monthly inspirational thought and reading suggestions? Join my mailing list! Sign up today at candlesutton.com.

God bless you for reading. I hope you will remain in His word so you can know truth from error and recognize His voice when He speaks. Grow in Him and hold firmly to the calling He places on you. There is no richer life than to do the work He gives.

Made in the USA
Middletown, DE
05 May 2022

65312745R00194